Havelock's Little Band

CHARLES NORTH

Havelock's Little Band

The Journal of an English Officer
in the Indian Mutiny of 1857

Charles North

LEONAUR

*Havelock's Little Band: the Journal of an English Officer
in the Indian Mutiny of 1857*
by Charles North

Published by Leonaur Ltd

Material original to this edition and this editorial selection
copyright © 2011 Leonaur Ltd

ISBN: 978-0-85706-561-2 (hardcover)
ISBN: 978-0-85706-562-9 (softcover)

http://www.leonaur.com

Publisher's Notes

Contents

Preface

No record whatever having been given of the progress of Havelock's little band, from its original formation as the Allahabad Moveable Column, in June, 1857, till its subsequent arrival at Lucknow—although the interval is fraught with the liveliest interest, embracing as it does the successful advance of the force on Cawnpore, its passage of the Ganges into Oude, and its . subsequent operations there—the writer has ventured to supply the deficiency by offering the following narrative. He has been actuated chiefly by a desire to testify his admiration of the hardy endurance and indomitable courage of that band, especially the 78th Highlanders, or Ross-shire Buffs, with whom he served as a volunteer, from the commencement of Havelock's campaign till its termination.

The narrative was not intended originally to be published, but to serve only as a memorial of some of those stirring events and scenes which passed before the author's eye. As it was written in the field during the hot and rainy seasons, between June and November, and at a time when the force was exposed to many hardships, and latterly to the want of tents, the author ventures to claim the indulgence of the reader, more especially as his own constant occupation and broken health allowed him little opportunity for bestowing care upon the composition.

London

August, 1858

CHAPTER 1

The Storm Begins

CALCUTTA, MAY 14TH, 1857

Coming events cast their shadows before. Just forty-one days since I bade *adieu* to the shores of merry England, and, though but a few hours have passed since I landed in the City of Palaces, it is, nevertheless, apparent to me that the native portion of the community is in an unwholesome state of ferment. Without laying claim to prescience, I was prepared in some measure for this; private letters having informed me, before I left England, that disaffection had manifested itself amongst the native troops of the honourable company. Where will it end?

MAY 16TH

I removed to the Royal Barracks, met my old friend Walters, and was admitted an honorary member of the mess of Her Majesty's 53rd Regiment. The storm begins!

News has arrived today from Meerut of the mutiny of the 3rd cavalry. Joined by the 11th, 20th, and 94th Native Infantry, they have broken into the gaol and liberated one thousand two hundred prisoners, including eighty-five convicted troopers of the 3rd, sentenced to penal servitude for refusing to use cartridges issued to them, and for which act of disobedience they were placed in irons in the presence of the entire troops, and committed to gaol.

On the policy of this step I abstain from comment. It is marked in fire and blood by the mutineers. The absence of the

European troops at divine service has favoured their designs. They have burnt their lines or huts, attacked and dismantled the bungalows of English officers, and murdered all they could lay hands on. A cantonment so extensive as Meerut afforded strange facility for the commission of such atrocities, as time must of necessity have elapsed before our troops could be collected to disperse the mutineers; the lines of the European cavalry being at some distance, and the staff occupying widely-scattered bungalows. The approach of night favoured the flight of the insurgents, who have taken the road to Delhi. Should the conflagration become general, as I apprehend, how are we prepared to resist it? Only two available regiments are in the Presidency; Her Majesty's 53rd, here at Fort William, and Her Majesty's 84th, brought from Burma, to overawe the mutinous 19th Native Infantry when disbanded at Barrackpore, probably to sow the seeds of disaffection as they dispersed. We have neither cavalry nor artillery; nor have we even a general officer. Such is the state of military preparation in Bengal.

According to the favourite system, European troops have been generally dispensed with, Cawnpore being garrisoned by a miserable detachment of Her Majesty's 32nd, and all the stations on the Grand Trunk road held by Sepoys.

MAY 27TH

Matters progress as usual here, despite the cloud of rebellion looming in the distance, and ready to burst upon the Presidency. The too apparent disloyalty of the native troops has not prevented the annual celebration of Her Majesty's birthday, in honour of which a ball has been given by the governor-general, and however much distrust is felt, none is expressed, and appearances are kept up.

Indeed the general opinion seems to favour the idea of partial rebellion rather than general disaffection, palpable as it is, notwithstanding the fact of the Sepoys at Allyghur and Ferozepore having followed the example of their brethren without offering violence to their officers or other Europeans. All classes seem pervaded by a feeling of panic, while the inertness on the part of those military authorities who ought to make arrangements to meet every exigency is remarkable.

JUNE 5TH

At length my representations have been attended to. I have gained permission to make the attempt to join my regiment (60th, Royal Rifles) at Meerut, distant from hence about nine hundred miles. The roads having been for some time impassable for private travellers, an escort is necessary; and tomorrow I am to accompany the headquarters of Her Majesty's 84th, under the immediate command of Captain Pakenham.

JUNE 6TH

I crossed with Her Majesty's 84th Regiment from Barrack-pore at six p.m., and awaited the 8.30 train to Ranee Gunge, one hundred and twenty-one miles from Calcutta. This I unfortunately missed, in consequence of the mismanagement of a railway official, but I followed in the goods train, and reached my destination four hours after the express. The heat during the forenoon was almost insufferable, especially to one newly arrived like myself.

At half-past four we exchanged the speed of steam for the tortoise-like progress of bullock wagons, heavy lumbering conveyances used for purposes of traffic, and drawn by bullocks, which, in too many instances, are both too small and weak for the great unwieldy carts they are condemned to draw; but such is the only means of transit, no military train being in existence.

The completion of a line of railway here would indeed be of incalculable importance; particularly at this season of the year, when troops are seldom either permitted or required to march, and when even the ordinary exercises and drills are dispensed with. I wish that those persons, whose duty it is to forward such improvements, were only exposed to the scorching, jolting, dust and glare, to which their supineness has unnecessarily doomed us.

June 8th

We halted at Taldunga, having absolutely accomplished the remarkable feat of twenty-five miles in fifteen hours; the ordinary *dak* bungalow, never intended to accommodate more than from five to ten persons, being our only resting-place, and shared alike by officers and men.

During the day we were joined by the lieutenant-colonel and staff of Her Majesty's 84th, who, more fortunate than we, travel in horse carriages in front of the troops. The duties of the commissariat department, in the absence of any of its officers, now devolve upon the officer commanding the troops, in the purchase and issue of the daily rations, leaving him but little time for needful repose.

June 14

With thirst unslaked, and black lips "baked," we reached Sherghotty, where we halted at the *dak* bungalow.

Never was a hotter day! The blood seemed to circulate like liquid fire through our veins, our eyes were dazzled by the glare, our limbs ached, and heads reeled from exposure; a canvas covering being the only kind used as curtains for those detestable wagons. Here I parted from my kind fellow travellers, Domenichetti of the 8th, or King's Regiment, Pakenham and Ayton, 84th, as, overcome by extreme fatigue, consequent upon night work, I was compelled to snatch a brief repose. My exertion to accelerate the progress of our wagons during the entire of our tedious march had been most strenuous and unremitting. I could not brook delay, when the necessity for speed was so imperious, and was unable philosophically to resign myself to the system of "*laisser aller.*"

I therefore undertook to facilitate our advance, in which my acquaintance with the native languages proved useful; though I have been often moved to ire by the apathy of the men, who give no assistance whatsoever, but stoically reconcile themselves to circumstances, and sleep night and day, if possible.

Good people, sitting at home at ease, you have no conception of the great difficulties to be encountered on the line of march in India, or you would raise your voices in exclamation against those who permitted their existence, instead of overcoming them. By employing a number of conductors of proper rank and energy to enforce promptitude, much time would be economised, and the troops prevented from encountering unnecessary exposure. The officer in charge would be spared a harassing duty, which, as a matter of course, would be both more correctly and efficiently performed by persons conversant with it, who should be posted at intervals along the road, for the superintendence of drivers and *coolies*, when employed.

June 15th

After a night's rest, I resumed my journey, which, owing to the kindness of a stranger in the civil service, I performed with ease and speed, as he brought me on in his carriage from Sherghotty to Benares. We travelled express, and found the line of road almost deserted by the villagers, who, terrified lest they might be punished for outrages perpetrated by the Sepoys, had dismantled their dwellings.

June 16th

At half past seven a.m., I reached the *dak* bungalow at Benares, shortly after the dispersion of the mutinous 37th Native Infantry and a small number of Sikhs under the guns of Major Olpherks, Her Majesty's 10th Foot and Madras Fusiliers. The Sikhs, it is alleged, were compelled to join in the mutiny of the 37th Native Infantry, in consequence of the irregular manner in which steps were taken to disarm that regiment on the parade ground by a commanding officer, incapacitated both by age and want of firmness from acting with that vigorous determination which the occasion required, and to which laxity of discipline had led. Strange to say, the officers of the 37th Native Infantry have asserted that the spirit of disaffection was excited in their corps by two companies of Her Majesty's 10th, belonging to the brigade. Should there be any truth in this report, nothing short of the grossest mismanagement could have led to such a result. All here is confusion and dismay; a large number of panic-stricken families have sought shelter in the mint-house, where they live in a most unenviable state of alarm, in which some of the troops doing duty participate. The exigency of the present crisis alone prevents me from exploring this wonderful city, which, from the little even that I have seen, appears to be one of remarkable interest.

All attempts at description would be utterly vain, farther than to observe that it is a strange jumble of meanness and magnificence; with narrow, tortuous streets, so narrow that no wheeled carriage larger than a Bath chair or perambulator might traverse them. The houses rise from two to six stories, many of which are built to project one above the other and meet that of the opposite side, so that the general characteristic of the streets is silence, dirt, and gloom. The windows are all very small.

Noble *ghats*, of the finest freestone, many of them elaborate in ornament, lead to the Ganges, which forms a magnificent bay in front of the city. These are interspersed with *sivalas*, or temples sacred to the various deities of Hindoo theology, superabounding in hands, heads, and hideousness. In the midst of the city rises a superb mosque, built by the Emperor Aurungzebe; to make room for which a fine Hindoo temple was sacrificed to Mahommedan intolerance.

There is also a beautiful temple by Chet'hee Sing, who in 1781 was driven from Benares for seeking to create disaffection to British rule; he was stripped of his authority a couple of years subsequently, and deprived of the dignity of rajah.

Should his spirit now hover near that place, in any of the various stages of metempsychosis incident to its final purgation, and retain the memory of former days, it must doubtless rejoice in the prevailing anarchy. One of the strangest features in the place is a hospital for the aged and infirm "of the male creation," as the somewhat euphuistic eloquence of Burke has designated animals; nor is this feeling of tenderness, resulting from belief in the transmigration of souls, confined to them alone, but is extended to the most loathsome insect life, reaching even to the foulest parasitic vermin, for the nourishment of which a certain number of beggars are retained.

Benares has been considered the chief seat of learning; it is of immense sanctity; consequently, extremely filthy.

June 17th

I left Benares by the steamer *Mirzapore*. The effect of the city from the deck was most picturesque; its *ghats* being crowded, as usual, with Mahommedans, Hindoos, and various other natives, bathing, dressing, praying, gesticulating, not to mention many wretched *fakirs*, woefully distorted, and redolent of cow dung, while slender minarets, domed mosques, and pinnacled temples heighten the novelty of the impression.

On board the *Mirzapore* was the headquarters of the Madras Fusiliers proceeding to Allahabad. The vessel, being heavily laden, took the ground repeatedly, which seemed a matter of utter indifference to its master, who, though under an advantageous contract with government, showed the utmost impassibility, and did not make the least effort to speed our advance. He evinced a total ignorance of his position with regard to the officer in command of the troops, and under whose orders he was directed to hold himself, and showed no energy except in giving expression to his wish "to return to Calcutta."

June 20th

About ten miles below Allahabad, the "mud-constant *Mirzapore*" again ran aground, and was passed by the steamer *Calcutta*, with the headquarters of Her Majesty's 84th. I got into a boat, followed and boarded this vessel, and landed at Allahabad next morning, having cast anchor during the night.

June 21st

The *Mirzapore* has just arrived, having been aground thirty hours. These are startling times. I have just heard of the dreary tragedy of the sixth of June, when the 6th Native Infantry, alone occupying this cantonment, burst into open mutiny, and murdered every officer who appeared on the parade ground.

The more effectually to secure their victims, they fixed upon the hour after tattoo for carrying their sanguinary designs into execution, sounded the alarm, and fired upon their officers as they appeared upon the ground; the mess-guard firing into the mess-room lest any should escape. A few, who were slightly wounded, attempted to save themselves by flying to the fort, but were pursued and murdered on the spot.

One officer, Captain Gordon, was saved by some Sepoys of this very regiment, who were friendly to him, and insisted on his preservation, placing him on a horse, and bidding him to fly.

Colonel Simpson, in command, also escaped to the fort. So persuaded was this latter officer of the fidelity of his regiment, that he lent no heed to the warning he received of its disaffection on the morning of that day, when the fact was communicated to him by the orderly-room clerk, a half-caste native. Fatal incredulity! All the private bungalows and military lines have been burnt down by the Sepoys in the cantonments. Nor is this all; they have seized two guns, which, by order of Colonel Simpson, were to have been conducted into the fort at nine p.m. on the evening of this tragedy. These guns were guarded by one hundred and fifty of the 6th Native Infantry, and were in charge of Lieutenant Harwood, Bengal Artillery, who, with other officers, represented the imprudence of this measure, and ventured to remonstrate, but in vain.

Under the peculiar circumstances, he might have used his own discretion, but shrunk from the responsibility of acting in contravention to a command issued for so late an hour. The immediate cause of this outbreak is attributed to an exaggerated account of the state of affairs at Benares.

How we retained the fort, garrisoned only by a single European detachment of invalid artillery and the Sikh regiment of Ferozepore, is really astonishing. Lieutenant Brazier, in command of the Sikhs, has held them in check by the most consummate tact, and proved himself both an efficient and courageous soldier.

The fort, which is built of red stone, rises proudly from the confluence of the rivers Ganges and Jumna, on the south and east; the land side is considerably elevated, quite regular, and consists of two bastions. It is about 2,500 yards in circuit, and on the sides near the rivers almost impregnable.

The arsenal is within the fort, and one of the largest in India. It contains a vast quantity of arms. Lieutenant-Colonel Neil, Madras Fusiliers, is commandant. His zeal and activity are unremitting. It was by his timely arrival at Benares, a few days since, that the mutiny was checked there, and the Europeans saved from the fury of the mutineers.

CHAPTER 2

To Cawnpore

JUNE 30TH

We left Allahabad, *en route* to Cawnpore, for the relief of General Sir Hugh Wheeler, who, with his small force, is hemmed in by the rebel army, and yet achieving wonders. Nana Sahib, the rajah of Bithoor, a Monathie, and our some-time friend, has assumed the chief command, and to the standard of this arch-rebel numbers are flocking.

Between him and the garrison of Cawnpore, a feeling of amity has hitherto existed, and he has been constant in the exercise of hospitality towards them. His present adverse conduct he justifies by some fictitious grievance. Our advanced column is commanded by Major Renaud, Madras Fusiliers, a man brave even to rashness. It consists of one hundred Irregular Cavalry, under Captain Palliser, two guns under Lieutenant Harwood, the Sikh Regiment of Ferozepore, and part of a movable column under formation by Brigadier-General Havelock, C.B., all full of spirit and eager to relieve our beleaguered countrymen from overwhelming odds, against which they bear up and struggle, too, so manfully. Courage, brave hearts, aid is at hand!

News has just arrived of the fall of Delhi. It was taken, on the 14th June, by the royal troops under General Sir Harry Barnard. The insurgents fought like fiends, and lost seven thousand in the desperate conflict. They maintained themselves to the last in the royal palace. This news will act as a salutary check upon the mutineers before Cawnpore.

Towards the close of the day, we halted at Moopteckeepore. The heat during our march was extremely trying—the more so, as we had to encounter a hot wind, which parched us like the breath of a furnace.

July 1st

We reached Koila, an unimportant village. During this line of march, some villages were fired; and any native found in arms, who could not prove his asserted innocence, was summarily hanged, such being the instructions under which we acted.

July 3rd

We received information from that most energetic and superior statesman. Sir Henry Lawrence, which caused us to halt here at Lohanda, four miles in advance. His present position is extremely critical—chief commissioner of Oude, and maintaining himself at Lucknow with very inferior numbers against the disbanded soldiery of the Oude irregular force, who have taken advantage of the present crisis to declare their independence of British rule, and proclaim their fidelity to the king of Oude, now a prisoner of the honourable company, and under strict surveillance at Calcutta.

July 4th

We marched to Kuttohan, seven miles, where we opened communication with a steamer on the Ganges, conveying a company of the Madras Fusiliers, with some artillery commanded by Captain Frazer from Allahabad, who is to cooperate abreast of this column. So great is the difficulty in obtaining carriage, that the force under Brigadier General Havelock has not yet marched from Allahabad.

July 7th

A discharge of heavy guns from the direction of the river has put us all on the *qui vive*. This we ascertained was occasioned by an unfortunate mistake on the part of the artillery on board, in opening fire from the steamer upon the village of a loyal *zemindar*, who had both protected and sheltered officers and their families of the mutinous Sepoy regiments.

A letter of explanation and apology has been sent to him *en route* to Allahabad, and he has been invited to open communication with our commander. The *zemindar*'s people have armed and followed the steamer, firing upon it from the banks, and compelling us to return the fire.

Intelligence has just been received that the city of Futtehpore (place of victory) two marches in advance, has been completely deserted, both by its inhabitants and the insurgents.

In this village (Kuttohan) a quantity of British railway property has been found; the houses in which it was discovered have been blown up, and a number of buried arms come to light. These we have secured.

JULY 8TH

We marched from Kuttohan, four and a half miles. For the past few days we have had constant rain, not a spot of dry ground for encamping upon. The flatness of the country renders it at a season like the present a complete swamp.

There being no choice, we pitched our tents near the line of railway, and found the premises a heap of ruins, the work of the mutineers. It was fortunate that no rain fell while we awaited the arrival of our baggage which came up but slowly. Had the orders not been so hurriedly issued much time would have been saved in its transit. The tents were of double weight, in consequence of their being saturated with rain, and were oppressively burdensome to the emaciated bullocks, scarcely able to crawl beneath their load. Two of the poor animals died from the ill-treatment which they received at the hands of some European soldiers.

Here I must pause to make a few remarks on what more particularly affects a column composed, like this, of various corps. I would suggest that every precaution necessary to enforce strict regularity should be taken; that the orders should be written, not verbally issued, and nothing be left doubtful or uncertain.

Prompt attention on the line of march is indispensable for the preservation of discipline, without which soldiers degenerate into an armed mob.

A commanding officer should consider nothing either trivial or unimportant which in the least affects the well-being of his men, whom he should save from fatigue as much as possible, so as to be able to act promptly and effectively when occasion requires. Judicious leading always inspires confidence, while vacillation or unsteadiness is fatal to it.

July 9th

We marched on Khanga, four and a-half miles, and halted again near the line of railway, beneath a tope of Mangoes, on ground better than that of the last two days, which was almost completely under water.

Fresh inconvenience, however, arose from the hurried orders of the preceding evening. It was quite dark when the baggage could be got upon the ground; there was no shelter for our men, and no mercy for the miserable bullocks, laden with wet tents; had we but started at dawn, all this might have been avoided, man and beast spared, and our advance to relieve the brave band at Cawnpore accelerated. According to an old law, "delays are dangerous." May they not prove so in the present instance.

July 10th

Well may I exclaim, grant me patience, for I feel sorely in need of the virtue. How tedious has our progress been to this place, Arrahpore, only four miles and a-half. When shall men learn foresight to provide for contingencies.

It is the old story. Experience must be the teacher, and dearly must her lessons, like all other good things, be paid for. By neglecting the military work of levelling a small piece of ground, which four men could easily have done in two hours, the advance of our carts has been greatly retarded through the obstruction in their route, and the wretched, ill-fed, over-worked bullocks have been doubly tasked.

Joyfully have I just heard of the advance of Brigadier-General Havelock to within four miles of this place, which he has accomplished with great celerity.

July 11th

We halted at Arrahpore. In the evening, I visited General Havelock's camp, and fortunately gained his permission to join the 78th Highlanders, or Ross-shire Buffs. Both officers and men look much fatigued and worn, having recently arrived from service in Persia. I am glad to say, there are but few in hospital—fine fellows. They are all in good spirits.

Sunday, July 12th

I joined General Havelock's column, and felt exceedingly gratified to receive his thanks for having recommended the halt at Lohanda, which he was pleased to call "a good service." Yet I cannot flatter myself that my opinion would have had the least weight, but for the timely arrival of instructions from that great man, Sir Henry Lawrence, thus pithily expressed—"Halt where you now stand, or, if necessary, fall back." His last intelligence, forwarded to us on what he believes to be reliable authority, is dreary in the extreme—*viz.*, "on the 28th of June, Cawnpore fell into the hands of the rebels, and that fine old man, Sir Hugh Wheeler, and his force, were all destroyed by an act of foul treachery on the part of the Nana."

When called upon to give my opinion, prior to the receipt of Sir Henry Lawrence's dispatch, I found myself considerably in the minority, but I did not speak unadvisedly. I had anxiously weighed the matter in my mind, and spoke not impulsively, but deliberately; I knew the insufficiency of our numbers, but now feel not a little pleased that such high authority as that of Sir Henry Lawrence supports my opinions. He forbade us to advance with less than two full English regiments and six guns— we had little more than four hundred Europeans and only two guns. Mine was a most trying position. I hope I may never again be similarly situated. Our daring commander was eager to push on, notwithstanding Sir Henry Lawrence's instructions from Lucknow, and orders diametrically opposite forwarded from Calcutta by Sir Patrick Grant, who assumes "that the report about the fall of Cawnpore is a fabrication, and therefore to push on thither." But as the senior officer present of Her Majesty's Service, I strenuously remonstrated against the vague instructions from Calcutta being complied with; the more particularly as I knew we should be reinforced on the morrow by General Havelock's column; and then, what evil looks, had I from old and young—but the courteous acknowledgment of my present commander amply compensates for foregone vexation.

CHAPTER 3

With the Highlanders

JULY 13TH

Yesterday, at one a.m., we formed a junction with General Havelock's column, and advanced towards Futtehpore, passing through Bellinda at seven a.m., and about five miles distant from thence.

There we halted to encamp; arms were piled in line, ground was taken up for each corps, and the weary, way-worn men, overcome by the oppressive heat and brilliant sunshine, lay down in groups, a little in the rear, anxiously expecting the arrival of the tents and baggage, which were close behind.

At this time our quarter-master general, Lieutenant-Colonel Tytler, was in front, making a reconnaissance towards the town of Futtehpore with the volunteer cavalry. It is probable that the enemy deceived himself as to the strength of our force, and imagined that he had merely the small band under Major Renaud to contend with; for no sooner did he see the reconnoitring party retire, than his first gun opened fire, and sent a round shot bowling along the road, upon the heels of our cavalry, riding stoutly to the line. In a moment the scene was changed, the assembly sounded, and the toil-worn men resumed their energy, sprung to their feet, unpiled arms, formed a line of columns, and advanced skirmishers.

The enemy, with his numerous cavalry, formed an imposing line as he bore down insolently upon us, confident of an easy victory, pushing forward two guns, and cannonading our front. Immediately our guns, Maude's Battery, posted in the middle of the road which formed our centre, roared defiance as they opened fire upon the advancing foe, while the Enfield rifles of the 64th poured in a shower of bullets from a copse at the left of the road; at either side of which lay swampy ground, increasing our difficulty, from being partly under water, rising from three to four feet, to retard our progress.

Scarce had our advance commenced, before three guns were descried by the light company of the 78th Highlanders. These had been deserted upon the road; on observing which they rushed impetuously onwards, while Maude's battery advanced at a rapid pace, firing with the most admirable precision, and closely followed by the light company of the 78th in an advance over three or four miles. The Enfield rifles of the 78th began taking long shots at the enemy as they retreated hurriedly through the town, which now became visible, its entrance barricaded by native carts, and apparently all the baggage of the mutineers.

Here, while running on with the skirmishers in eager pursuit, I met with a severe accident, little heeded at the time, owing to the intense excitement of the fray.

A bullock lashed to fury by the pain of its wounds (it had been struck with a round shot) rushed from the town, and as it dashed violently against me, lifted me from the ground, and, striking at me, fortunately between its horns, flung me to some distance. A kind-hearted Highlander who, "with more chivalry than wisdom," interposed to save me, was also bowled over in every acceptation of the term. The blow was " stunning," yet, sustained by an impetuous impulse of volition, I was quickly on my feet, and dashed off at a double in pursuit of the enemy, as he bolted through the village, sending an occasional random shot at his relentless pursuers.

The Light company of the 78th, and a company of the 64th, boldly forced an entrance through the network of carts, ingeniously placed to interrupt our progress, and carried the town— ignominiously deserted by the mutineers.

Thus the battle of Futtehpore was decided by the intrepid advance of our guns and skirmishers; the reserve columns being far in the rear, owing to the impediments of the ground. Up to this time the troops had marched for twenty-four miles without a meal to sustain their over tasked energies; yet, at eleven o'clock a.m., Futtehpore was ours. No casualties had occurred during the fight: but several died from sun-stroke.

And now that the necessity for exertion no longer existed, a sudden faintness seized upon me while marching through the town. In vain I strove to resist it. Overpowered by severe pain resulting from the contusion which I had received in my encounter with the bullock, I sank down insensible. Nor did I recover consciousness for some time, when, to my surprise, I found myself lying on a bed in the gaol, whither I had been borne by a corporal and private of the 84th, who were bathing my head and side with the utmost kindness, while some medical officers hung anxiously over me. But the most effectual remedy was a bottle of champagne, for which I was indebted to the kind feeling of Lieutenant-Colonel Tytler, who had been presented with it a little before by one of the men, but who forgot his own thirst and need of refreshment for my benefit. Never was drink more reviving or stimulant more required, and I truly appreciate the self-denial of the gift.

I was the only person hurt at Futtehpore, with the exception of Butterworth, the Highlander who had attempted to save me. We both suffered from the same cause. My escape on this occasion I hope I may remember with thankfulness.

In Futtehpore a vast deal of various sorts of plunder, with some treasure, has been found.

Not till eight o'clock p.m. did our brave troop get a meal, and then after a fast of fourteen hours, during which time they marched and fought exposed to the fierce heat of an Indian summer, when in all cantonments troops are kept in their barracks, and forbidden to expose themselves. Towards the termination of the battle of Futtehpore an incident occurred, which I omitted to mention, and shall record here.

When General Havelock saw the mutineers in retreat towards the town, which they approached in confusion, he addressed himself to one of his staff, the brave Moorsom, of the 52nd, and said: "I should like to see the irregulars draw blood."

They (the 13th) were ordered immediately to charge, but all hung back, with the exception of a dozen, led on by Captain Palliser in gallant style. Ten were killed, and the rage and disappointment of this officer was not less than the occasion merited. Our infantry received orders to fire upon the recusants on the spot, which would only have been a just punishment for such baseness; this order, hastily given, was as hastily rescinded—mistaken leniency.

July 14th

At daybreak we advanced towards the village of Calleanpore, and met small parties of rebel cavalry on our left flank, with whom we had engaged the preceding day. They showed a great inclination to fall upon our baggage. To prevent the execution of this design, our line was formed in echelon of wings, the left in rear.

Some heavy firing took place, during which the Madras Fusiliers on the right gave the rebels a severe lesson on the efficiency of the rifled musket; for though unaccustomed to use it at so long a range, their practice was excellent. Major Renaud, while directing the advance of the skirmishers of his corps, and exposing himself unnecessarily, was most severely wounded, together with some of his men.

But the telling effect of our guns under Captain Maude, the Invalid Artillery, and two guns under Lieutenant Haward, on the left centre, together with the withering fire of our sharpshooters, forced the enemy to abandon his position before noon, when the troops halted for rest and such refreshment as was attainable, viz., grog and biscuit.

Of these we partook beneath the welcome shelter of some friendly topes of mangoes.

Most grateful was their shade, inviting to repose after recent exposure to the fiery sunbeams, which seemed literally to pierce and seethe the brain. The relief was unimaginable.

Here I must pause to express my commendation and appreciation of the kind brotherly feeling of my brave companions in arms, the 78th Highlanders. Never upon any occasion did they omit to draw my grog ration for me. This consideration for the wants of their officers is conspicuous through the ranks of this distinguished regiment, with which I regard it as a privilege to serve as a volunteer.

Generally speaking, men placed in similar circumstances are more inclined to attend to themselves than to care for others, and such good feeling on the part of subordinates bears ample testimony of the interest which, when it really exists and is carried out practically, must ever conduce to the preservation of discipline. To quote from Highest authority, "a house divided against itself cannot stand," so it is with a regiment; kindness begets kindness, and harmony is the result of mutual interdependence.

Our rest was of brief duration, for the assembly again sounded; the entire force resumed their arms and moved forward, soon to join in a line of columns, guns in the centre. This move was hailed by our dauntless little band with a stirring British cheer, which made the welkin ring, as it marked their enthusiastic approval of our General's readiness again to engage the mutineers, discovered once more in position in the distance at Pandoo Nuddie; a *wallah*, or river, then almost dry, and spanned by a narrow bridge of masonry, defended by entrenchments, and having two huge guns in position.

It had been contemplated to force the passage of the stream, but the bridge offered a more favourable point of attack, though the entire position of the enemy seemed capable of affording most obstinate resistance to any attempt we should make to carry it, and it was understood that he would defend it to the last. But nothing could resist the impetuosity of our troops, or damp the ardour of their leaders, predetermined to succeed, and burning to relieve our unfortunate countrywomen and helpless children from their durance at Cawnpore. As our columns of attack took up their ground in continuous line, a well-directed fire opened upon them from the enemy, who had marked this range upon the telegraph posts, and calculated with some accuracy our point of formation for attack. Several of our men were wounded, and a fine fellow, a Highlander, was shot dead in my front, half of his head having been taken off by a round shot.

The men were ordered to lie down for a few minutes, until they advanced in line, supporting our guns and skirmishers, who moved hastily to the front, while the enemy's position was at times hidden from our view, because of the irregularities of the ground.

As our column advanced towards the bridge, the enemy opened an effective fire, which caused it to deploy, while, animated by his accustomed daring, Maude's battery dashed resolutely up to within three hundred yards of the bridge, when his bullets produced their wonted effect. Meantime, the Madras Fusiliers suddenly closed, rushed boldly to the onslaught, carried the bridge in gallant style, and captured the two guns by which it was defended.

This was enough for the enemy, who completely lost heart, and despite his advantageous position and superior numerical force, only thought of getting off; a manoeuvre rapidly effected by him, and to which our want of Cavalry mainly contributed.

In subsequently crossing the bridge, we discovered traces of a vain attempt on his part to blow it up. The battle of Pandoo Nuddie was the second affair in which everything was won by our Artillery and skirmishers, who, by their effective use of the Enfield rifle musket, struck terror into the hearts of the mutineers; no steady resistance having been offered by them to its unerring fire. Indeed its length of range seemed utterly to discompose and fill them with terror.

Thus closed the 15th July.

During twelve hours our troops had been under arms and twice engaged, and their endurance tested to the uttermost. The scorching sun glared down its unpitying rays upon their arms, which glittered with intolerable radiance, till the brain reeled and eyeballs ached with the intensity of that dazzling sheen.

Yet their indomitable energy rose superior to every trial—instinct with the dignity of manhood, they uttered no complaint, but bore on nobly. Night had again closed, when their long fast was terminated by a meal.

Our casualties amounted to twenty-five killed and wounded; the enemy could have suffered but little, as he engaged us from a distance, and rapidly retired before us.

Our first battle, Futtehpore, it would seem, has checked his arrogance and damped his courage. We have captured four of his guns, including the two taken by the Madras Fusiliers, in this affair of Pandoo Nuddie; making in all sixteen since the 12th of July. We are now twenty-four miles distant from Cawnpore.

CHAPTER 4

The Battle for Cawnpore

JULY 16TH

Soon after daylight we marched towards Kullianpore, where information reached us that the mutineers were in position at the distance of a few miles.

A halt having been ordered to enable the baggage to come up and the troops to breakfast, we eagerly sought the shade of some umbrageous trees, which spread a kindly shelter between us and the intense sunshine.

Here we gladly rested, while our volunteer horse, with some infantry, took a post in advance to watch the movements of the enemy.

On the arrival of the baggage, all set busily to work; cooking was commenced, and breakfast was prepared. Wearied as we were from yesterday's operations and today's march, we duly appreciated this refreshment, which was indeed acceptable. We had, according to our usual custom since the fighting began, snatched what sleep we could while waiting for the baggage.

At two o'clock p.m. we re-commenced our march, leaving our baggage on the ground—for the defence of which due measures had been taken by the directions of General Havelock. Immediately before we started, a supply of porter had been issued, and the pernicious effects of this heavy drink were too speedily manifest; for, as the men advanced under a broiling sun, numbers fell out of the ranks and lay motionless upon the roadside, utterly insensible.

No sooner had we arrived at a village, situate at the junction of two roads, one of which leads to the cantonments of Cawnpore, than the enemy appeared posted; his batteries commanding our line of route.

On perceiving this, our force made a flank march, under cover of a tope or grove of mangoes, which was filled by the Madras Fusiliers skirmishing. We debouched for some distance in an open column of companies, and encircled the left flank of the enemy. This movement was for some time unsuspected by the enemy, as the intervening groups of trees screened it from his observation; but no sooner did he become aware of it, than the utmost excitement prevailed in his lines. As we made our advance, he poured in a heavy fire of shot and shell upon us from all his guns.

Most fortunately for us the range was too high, though our column of infantry was greatly exposed to this fire, from having been unsupported by our batteries; the progress of which was woefully tedious, because of the freshly ploughed ground, through which our overworked gun-bullocks toiled laboriously. Our brave General led this movement in person, and it was one that took the enemy completely by surprise, as it left him powerless to counteract the advance.

The guns followed slowly as the line was again re-formed at right-angles with its previous advance; and the moment seemed to have arrived for testing the mettle of the gallant Highlanders, who, as they advanced in an unwavering line, were ordered to charge a battery of four guns, which had occasioned us great annoyance, and which our artillery were not ready to silence. It was in vain that showers of grape fell thick and fast among them. A volley of defiance and a spirit stirring cheer, a cheer that brought dismay into the hearts of the mutineers, were returned, and the guns were ours.

The enemy retired in confusion. Our left wing, 64th, 84th, and Sikh Regiment, were in hot pursuit towards a village in front of our left flank, where more guns were captured. The right wing made a sweep to the right, where two guns were found deserted. These they seized; and the plain being again apparently abandoned, and the artillery still in the rear, we halted for their arrival.

About this time, the quarter-master sergeant of the Highlanders, a fine, stalwart man, and several others, incapable of resisting the fiery rays of the sun, dropped down suddenly dead.

As the troops rejoined from the pursuit, we discovered that the enemy had re-occupied a village sheltered by groves of mangoes. On our rounding it, a cannonade was opened from this line, distant from the cantonment of Cawnpore about one mile, and from whence he had been reinforced. We therefore shifted our ground a little, as our artillery came up but slowly, in consequence of having been obliged to diverge from the direct road, and cross through heavy broken ground; a work of difficulty to our overworked, ill-fed cattle. Meantime, the cannonade became more concentrated, killing and wounding many men in our left centre during the advance.

Our noble general seemed gifted with ubiquity, as, scornful of danger, confronting death, and burning with the lust of victory, he was present wherever most needed, urged onward by the soldier's stern sense of duty. Again, the clear tone of his peculiar voice raised to highest pitch the courage of his men, as he hurried towards the Highlanders and said: "Come, who'll take this village—the Highlanders or 64th," looking to the latter, as he addressed them, with the utmost coolness.

There was no pause to answer. The spirit of emulation was a flame in every breast, kindled by his calm words. We (the Highlanders), eager for approval, went off quickly in the direction indicated; moving steadily onwards in a direct, compact line, its front covered by the Light company, and pushing the enemy's skirmishers through the village, from whence they were compelled by us to fly. The Madras Fusiliers, by whom our line to the right was prolonged, drove them from the plantation.

Scarcely had these advantages been gained, when we suddenly observed a strong body of mutineers, with numerous cavalry and guns in position, bugles and drums going, as if to advance in the form of a semicircle, which menaced our right. They were only some yards distant, and a fresh engagement was inevitable. It was now past sunset, and our proximity to the enemy's new position exposed us so much to the fire of his heavy guns, that the troops who first appeared in his front were compelled to lie down; whilst in the centre of our left wing, 64th and 84th, several were killed in advancing across the enemy's line, so grievously were they exposed to the raking fire of a twenty-four pounder.

The augmented numbers of our adversary rendered our position most critical. Our artillery was still in the rear, our strength diminished by numerous cases of sunstroke which had occurred during the day, nor had the Sikh Regiment yet come up to our relief. We could not have mustered more than nine hundred men, and were totally destitute of cavalry; while the enemy, strong in this arm, enveloped our flanks in the form of a crescent.

When lying on the ground, I observed the Madras Fusiliers, commanded by their gallant leader, Major Stephenson, advancing in close column, unaware of impending destruction, which I comprehended at a glance. I sprung to my feet from the narrow ridge of earth on which I had been lying with the Highlanders, and rushing across the plain, warned him of the danger which the waning light concealed from him, as his noble regiment advanced in this formation, to which either a round shot or discharge of grape would have proved of deadly effect.

On receiving my warning, he quickly deployed into line, and lay down with us upon the ground.

With increasing darkness, shadows lengthened, which added to the imposing effect of the rebel line, seeming yet more dense and numerous; drums and trumpets insolently sounding the advance in quick repetition.

General Havelock, who had just had his horse shot under him, now appeared, boldly riding a hack, the only man who dared raise his head—so close and thick was the fire that rained upon us. He instantly, with clear and firm tone, gave the order, "the line will advance." Hardly were the words spoken, when a feeling of confidence inspired every breast, and displaced the overwhelming weight of uncertainty and doubt engendered by inaction. Up sprung our thinned line, not amounting to nine hundred strong; their quick pace accelerated by the double, they bounded onward.

At the word "forward," the space between the hostile lines was so inconsiderable, that a general melee seemed inevitable, the odds being fearfully against us. But to this act of intrepidity in our general his troops worthily responded. Their ardour and enthusiastic daring had mounted to that height almost resembling frenzy; acknowledging no obstacle, and overleaping every barrier, their impetuosity was irresistible. Hurrah! Well done, brave 64th, the very gun from which we suffered so severely is captured! Away! Away! Across the plain, like the shifting figures in a panorama, the cowardly rebels disappeared; our troops following in hot pursuit till we reached the verge of the cantonment. Here we halted in view of the artillery barracks, which lay in our front. We had neither tents, rations, nor grog. But we had the commendation of our General, and the glowing terms in which he addressed us proved how truly he appreciated our ardour.

Like all lofty natures superior to egotism, he seemed to forget the greatness of his own example while recognizing our prowess. Well is such a leader calculated to inspire confidence, secure esteem, and lead us on to victory; or, if need be, to death! He it was who had led this most determined onslaught, in which darkness shrouded our reduced numbers, the Highlanders in the centre (their usual position) cautioning each other not to fire, as the general was in front; but for this, they would have poured a withering volley on their retreating foe. Our casualties now amounted to a hundred and five, including four days' fighting, during which we had captured twenty-three pieces of artillery.

CHAPTER 5

The Tragedy

July 17th

We arrived at Cawnpore. Nothing can be more cheerless or desolate than the view presented by the company's ground; the most conspicuous and thrilling objects being the two barrack buildings so unhappily chosen by Sir Hugh Wheeler after the mutiny of all the native troops at this station on the 6th June.

There could scarcely have been a more fatally exposed position. The roofless, on all sides, but absolutely commanded by the new barracks, built in echelon along their front, and affording complete cover to their assailants. Outside the entrenchments, a mere furrow, are a few rifle-pits. In another place, the ground is excavated as a means of protecting the poor women from the fire of the enemy, who, against this exposed position, had actually commenced to open parallels.

So long as hope remained to the defenders, they did not hesitate to make the most desperate sorties to capture the guns of the mutineers. Never can their courage be impugned. So few were the Europeans, and so destitute were they of men to work the guns, that they were served alternately by those who tried, with fruitless perseverance, to put down the fire of their treacherous and savage foe, to whose batteries these devoted buildings were easy targets.

Two only of that doomed British garrison survive—Lieutenants Delafosse and Thompson, who contrived to escape.

They joined the force under General Havelock on the march.

Their sufferings have been severe, and their preservation may be ascribed to the kindness of a native landowner, who, on hearing of their extraordinary trials, after escaping from the fire poured into the boats in which they were permitted to embark, sheltered them. Truly, indeed, may I exclaim in the words of the immortal bard:

There is a providence that shapes our ends,
Rough hew them as we will.

For despite my strenuous exertion and my urgent request for permission to accompany a detachment of Bengal Fusiliers, *en route* to Cawnpore from Calcutta, under the command of Lieutenant Glonville of that corps, I was peremptorily refused; which, at the time, occasioned me much irritation and impatience. Vain, blind mortal! I did not then see the hand of the Almighty outstretched to hold me back from the foul impending massacre, while now I humbly acknowledge the merciful interposition.

What conflicting passions tore our hearts and roused us to vengeance, as we learnt the cruel tale of the martyrdom of our hapless country-women and their tender babes. On the 15th July the sacrifice was consummated.

Tortured by the fierce thirst for revenge, and penetrated by the sense of their sufferings, strange wild feelings awoke within us. Panting, eager, maddened, we sped onwards to the dreary house of martyrdom, where their blood was out-poured like water; the clotted gore lay ankle deep on the polluted floor, and also long tresses of silken hair, fragments of female wearing apparel, hats, boots; children's tiny boots and toys were scattered about in terrible confusion. In a little book of daily prayers, which was picked up, was the following affecting inscription:

27th June, left the boats

Also:

7th July, went as prisoners to Salvador House, fatal day!

The dates and days of the week were entered up to the first

week of this month (July), a cross being marked up to the 6th, corresponding with a similar cross at every daily prayer, which ends at the flyleaf with the words:

For darling mamma, from her affectionate daughter,
Isabella Blair

Nor was this the only sight of horror that awaited us. More appalling still, there was the deep and narrow well within the same enclosure, choked with the mangled remains of those fair and helpless beings.

But this is no subject to dwell upon, and for the fiends who perpetrated the savage deed, a fiery retribution is at hand. We learn from the reports of the shopkeepers in the *bazaar,* as well as from the statement of others, that twelve thousand Sepoys held Cawnpore, who not only failed in resisting the advance of our determined little band, scarce amounting to nine hundred, but utterly abandoned this extensive station, which presents innumerable points of defence. Such is the terror inspired by our successful advance, nor would this be so surprising if our adversary was unskilled in the art of war. Trained, however, like ourselves to British discipline, greatly superior to us in number, and inured to the climate as children of the soil, it would almost seem as if a coward conscience whispered to him of vengeance, and drove him to flight.

We had been for several hours without food, but stimulated no less than horrified by the scene of the fearful catastrophe which I have recorded, we were quite unconscious of the want.

We now hurried onward towards some buildings which remained standing, and which had been used as sheds for cavalry. Here we gladly sheltered ourselves, as this was the first time of our having a roof over our heads since the 30th June, when we left Allahabad, a period of seventeen days. Yet during this time we had been exposed day and night to varied alternations, incident both to the climate and the season of the year.

At one time, we felt almost burnt or parched by the rays of a tropical sun. At another, we were drenched by the pouring rain, which chilled us to the bone, and flooding the earth beneath

38

our feet, rendered our footing insecure. All this added to the difficulties of our march, and tested our powers of endurance.

July 18th

Another deadly foe has entered the lists against us—one which makes the bravest among us shudder; for even those who in the battle-field were insensible to fear, even when the fatal ball whizzed past, winged with deaths now shudder at the name of cholera.

Our indefatigable adjutant-general, Captain Steuard Beatson, has succumbed to its deadly influence. Poor fellow, he struggled against the insidiousness of dysentery, up borne by the sense of duty till he was overcome by this fatal malady, which the damp reeking atmosphere, combined with over-exertion, speedily developed.

Another also departed—poor Currie, of the 84th, from the effects of a ghastly wound received in yesterday's conflict, and yet another still, the zealous, daring Renaud, Madras Fusiliers, whose courage and fortitude were proverbial!

He sank rapidly after the amputation of his left leg above the knee. I had gone to see him, found him in cheerful spirits, hoped for his ultimate recovery, and now he is not. Sad realities of ruthless war!

Chapter 6

Wheeler & Nana

CAMP, CAWNPORE, JULY 18TH

The rapidity with which events of the most stirring interest crowd upon each other, in every exciting variety, renders me forgetful of noting circumstances of minor import, however worthy of record they may be, as illustrative of the scenes amid which I move, and the persons amongst whom I live.

One conversant with human nature has said, "Sweet are the uses of adversity;" and truly the adverse influences, against which our little band struggles so manfully, seem to have developed extraordinary greatness of mind and wonderful powers of endurance.

With what cheerfulness, hunger, thirst, fatigue, and exposure are encountered and overcome in the face of danger. Not a word of repining is heard, although discomfort and privation are no longer comparative, but positive and absolute, I question, indeed, whether equal fortitude was to have been found in the Spartan of old. Could our friends at home but imagine what we endure, they would shrink from the contemplation, so painful would be the mere idea of those realities we contend against.

Strange how the ludicrous trenches upon the sublime! Never shall I forget the alarm that was spread on the night of the 16th, when, worn out by excitement of mind and overpowered by fatigue of body, we lay down to sleep in the arms of victory; but scarce had refreshing sleep descended on our fevered , eyelids, when a hasty shout ran through our lines that the enemy was upon us. They who heard the alarm sprung immediately to arms and awoke their comrades, myself among the number. We prepared to encounter the enemy, but we had already given him too severe a lesson of British prowess for him so soon to re-appear, and we speedily discovered that the disturbers of our slumber were no more formidable assailants than loose horses, several of which were galloping about the camp.

Early yesterday the execrable monster, Nana Sahib, retreated towards Bithoor, his stronghold, where it was understood he would make a determined resistance, it being a place of considerable strength and easily defended. His exit from Cawnpore was marked by a salute, such as those who heard it cannot easily forget. It did not consist of the mere formality of a given number of guns, but of the explosion of the entire magazine. This was of course a tremendous affair; the ground beneath us heaved and shook as if rent by the throes of an earthquake, and the air was darkened by the debris. It is said by the *bazaar* people that this has been the work of a holy man, a relation of the Nana's.

And now Bithoor, the very stronghold of the miscreant, is in our possession. It is some ten or twelve miles distant from hence. Not a single shot has it cost us. Major Stephenson and his fine regiment of Madras Fusiliers, on entering the place, found it abandoned by the Nana, who, with no fewer than five thousand armed followers, and forty-five guns in position, to dispute our advance, has remembered that the better part of valour is discretion, and acting on this principle, has suffered Bithoor to fall into our hands without the expenditure of any more gunpowder than what had exploded when the magazine blew up.

Fifteen guns have been captured, and some carriages and other valuable property found, which this wretch had abandoned in his ignominious flight.

JULY 19TH

The heavy and frequent rain incident during this monsoon weather makes writing a matter of difficulty. The ploughed ground beneath one's feet is a regular swamp. *Water, water everywhere!*

A dry jacket has been a luxury unknown to us for many days. We cannot find a dry corner wherein to sleep, while the number of frogs which luxuriate in this humid atmosphere is astonishing. They are great, unsightly, bloated-looking creatures; I have not made up my mind whether the large black frogs, streaked and fretted with dun colour, or the dingy yellow, variegated with black, are the most disagreeable. My presence does not seem to discompose them in the least.

They either flounder about in the little pools on my floor to their heart's content, or rest panting on the saturated earth; their round, shining eyes fixed on me at times, as if fascinated. Dysentery and cholera continue to increase. It is lamentable to see our fine fellows smitten by those dire scourges, to which the peculiar state of the atmosphere, superadded to fatigue and privation, predisposes them. The long fasts, too, which we have been obliged to endure, must encroach on bodily strength. Our last was of twenty one hours' duration, *viz.*, from noon on the 16th July, till 9 a.m. the following day. During this interval, not a man in our force had any refreshment, and at the end of these twenty-one hours, the meal served to them was of the most meagre description. Still there was not a murmur in their ranks. Supplies here are at present very scanty; and though brought into camp by the affrighted shopkeepers who have been hitherto accustomed to gain a livelihood by their dealings with Europeans, and who still continue to part with their goods on most advantageous terms, it is not very easy for the purchasers to secure them; indeed, if the owners do not escort the purchasers to their own tents, some greedy stragglers will endeavour to seize on the supplies purchased as a lawful prize; the laws of *meum* and *tuum* being at present in abeyance—*chacun pour soi*, the dominating influence.

July 22nd

I have been appointed to act as deputy judge advocate. I have no objection to the staff if serving upon it does not; prevent me from being useful in other matters more agreeable to my inclinations. Nothing can be more distasteful to me than a life of inactivity; during the present crisis it would be unendurable. As military lawyer, I believe I am justified in assuming that I shall have little employment: for there is almost an absence of crime in this brave little band.

Had one regiment only, like any of those which compose this band of Havelock's, been present here with Sir Hugh Wheeler, he might have made a stand till the arrival of relief. Poor victim of hope deferred, as much as of infernal treachery, he had been led to believe that reinforcements would have been sent to his aid by the 15th June. Relying on this fatal belief, he selected the buildings nearest to the direct road from Allahabad, from whence the relieving troops were expected to advance. Hence his exposed position. What eager, agonised looks must have been turned to that road, as day after day swept past, and reinforcements came not, and the hopes of the slender, over tasked garrison became fainter and fainter, while bodily strength wasted away, and, in addition to the savage foe, hunger also glared upon them.

What wonder that reason tottered, and credulity awoke and ' whispered of the Nana's foregone hospitality, the intimate relations which had originally subsisted between him and the beleaguered few, and his incapacity to betray trust reposed in his honour.

And so they fell into the snare, and tender-hearted women learned their own tenacity of life in looking on the extinction of life in the partners of their existence, and bore the dreadful memory, seared into their hearts, till their own martyrdom was consummated. The blood of those innocents cries out from the earth in reprobation of a system, which, from its slothfulness, led to this catastrophe, and which is totally at variance with the progress of modem civilization.

July 23rd.

Now a work of severe trial opens to us. We are about to cross the Granges, a mile wide here, much swollen by the incessant rain, and against an extremely strong current; our small steamer and a few native boats being the only means of transit. But Lucknow is to be succoured immediately by our shadow of an army, insufficient in itself to cover even Cawnpore, destitute of cavalry, horse artillery, or horse battery, and without a reserve between Cawnpore and Calcutta. Such are the instructions of the government, and such the means provided by the same authority, both for carrying out the instructions, *viz.*, the immediate relief of Lucknow, and also for holding the vast tract of territory between this and Calcutta!

The enterprise is a desperate one, and it will be seen whether a force so weak as ours can do more than make the attempt. The entire population of Oude is against us. Therefore we may anticipate the most stringent opposition; particularly as its people are remarkably warlike, much attached to their former rulers, and always opposed to our encroachment on their territory. They have not been brought into subjection to us by the sword of the warrior; their territory has merely been annexed by a stroke of the pen. This annexation was considered at the time an able piece of statesmanship, but it has since borne the bitter fruit of disaffection.

As the causes of the present mutiny are analysed, it becomes evident that the cause alleged, viz., the issue of Enfield rifle-cartridges, is utterly without foundation.

CHAPTER 7

Across the Ganges

JULY 25TH

Amidst torrents of rain, the 84th, 78th Highlanders, and 64th crossed the Ganges to cover the transport of our commissariat stores, which will occupy several days. Meantime our troops must live as best they can in a swamp, without means of shelter. Our desperate enterprise must not be hampered with the carriage either of tents or bedding, which we have left behind us at Cawnpore. Nothing can exceed the zeal and efficiency of Lieutenant-Colonel Tytler, our quartermaster general. His energy is untiring, as he personally superintends at the *ghat*, a ferry, the transport of men, horses, and stores—a work of some hours daily, in which he is assisted by other officers of his department, equally on the alert, and working night and day.

JULY 26TH.

The troops suffer severely on this swampy ground, which we have been obliged to occupy; unfortunately, there is no choice for us. Wet and cold bring an increase of dysentery.

My side and shoulder ache severely, and at times I find respiration painful. This is said to have resulted from the contusion which I received in my adventure with the bullock at the battle of Futtehpore. Today, we advanced to Mungurwar, occupied by some villagers, a good position, commanding the plain through which our route lies. We are now quartered in native huts, where we shall remain till our Commissariat enables us to advance.

Melancholy to relate, dysentery and cholera, occasioned by exposure and hard fare, have increased to such an extent amongst us that we are, of necessity, compelled to send the sick back to Cawnpore, where Brigadier Neil, with a detachment of less than two hundred and fifty men, commands. Such is the force he possesses to hold Cawnpore! While ours amounts to 1777 of all ranks, with ten guns.

July 29th

At half-past five a.m., we advanced towards Oonao, a distance of six miles; the villages *en route* being most obstinately defended from loop-holes and guns in position, which contested our progress. The fire upon the General and his Staff has been severe, and Lieutenant Seton, his Aide-de-camp has been badly wounded.

Between the village and town of Oonao is a space by which our column diverged, again to find the enemy advantageously posted in the plain beyond. From the manner in which he had chosen his position, we had no other alternative than to attack him in front; he being defended on his right by a wide swamp, which interposed a natural barrier between us. His advance was drawn up in a garden or enclosure, much resembling a bastion, while his remaining troops found a comparatively secure shelter in the loop-holed houses of a village, communicating by a narrow passage with the town, which lay on our right, something less than a mile distant; a position quite impossible for us to turn, in consequence of the inundated state of the country, owing to the heavy rams.

The 78th Highlanders and Madras Fusiliers, with two guns, commenced the attack, animated by their wonted spirit, and poured an effective fire upon the enemy, which drove him from the enclosure; but we suffered severely from a withering fire, poured upon us from the loop-holed houses in our approach to the village, till Colonel Wilson brought up the brave 64th to our relief; which turned the scale in our favour. Here some acts of bravery were performed, impossible to describe, as they border so much on the marvellous. Foremost in heroic daring was an Irishman named Patrick Cavanagh, a private of the 64th Regiment, whose conspicuous gallantry on this occasion was worthy of the Paladins of old and the admiration of all. He fell, literally hewn to pieces by the enemy; had he survived, he would have been recommended for the Victoria Cross.

In this our first encounter with the warlike people of Oude, we met with much more sustained opposition than upon any former occasion, and notwithstanding our having set fire to their village, they still resolutely defended themselves; but we were not to be foiled; we succeeded in capturing two of their guns, and debouched by the narrow passage which connects the village with the town of Oonao, where we formed line and discovered the enemy, who had rallied and assembled in great force, with infantry, guns, and cavalry, prepared to resist us. Having formed into echelons of detachments and batteries, we attacked them, captured their guns, and finally routed both their infantry and cavalry. Throughout this engagement, a large body of the Nana's troops threatened our left flank, but did not dare to come to an engagement.

In this action, Lieutenant Boyle, 78th Highlanders, while seeking to dislodge some religious fanatics from one of the houses in the village defended by matchlock men, received a severe wound.

During this time I had been in command of the rear-guard; I had been left in total ignorance of the column having diverged; indeed no intelligence whatsoever had reached me; but no sooner had our baggage reached the entrance of the village than I became aware of its arrival.

Now although our baggage was limited as to quantity, yet it formed a line of considerable length, and the number of heavy wagons required for the transport of Commissariat stores, together with a string of *palanquins* and *dhoolies* for sick and wounded, chiefly casualties of the day, seriously impeded our progress, and rendered our position the more critical. For a single moment, the entire body seemed panic-stricken; they wavered, and began to retire. Perceiving this, I instantly extended a short distance to either flank the few infantry under my command, with peremptory orders to shoot the first camp follower who attempted to go to the rear, got the *palanquins* and *dhoolies* with sick and wounded on the flank of my large wagons, and turning to the foremost elephant-driver, who seemed intent on effecting a safe retreat, threatened to shoot him on the spot if he did not immediately advance. This produced the desired effect; he seemed to think it safer to risk the possibility of the enemy's fire, than certain death from the muzzle of my heavy pistol, aimed at him; its silent appeal was eloquent to persuade, and once more the entire train was in motion.

Fortunately, we fell in with the Sikh regiment of Ferozepore, halted in the village. I took advantage of this circumstance, and aided them with guns to clear it. So brisk was the fire poured upon us, that it is not surprising our camp followers manifested feelings of alarm; but the guns of my escort opened upon the enclosure from whence we were annoyed, and with good effect, for I succeeded in passing the entire convoy without the loss of a single driver or any of the cattle. Unfortunately, one of my gunners was killed by a shot from a loop-hole, and this was my only casualty.

The column, meantime, was two miles in advance; it halted upon a swampy plain, partially drying up beneath the influence of intense sunshine, and wreathed in exhalations more or less noxious. There we joined it.

The difficulties which I had to encounter in forwarding this baggage were extreme, requiring the most constant and strenuous exertion, as well as the exercise of absolute authority on my part; but my efforts were crowned with the most complete success, and not a single case of desertion had occurred *en route*.

How I came to have been detached for that particular duty, command of the rear-guard, on that day, I know not; but so it was; though contrary to the express commands of the General, whom I ought to have attended. However, on his receiving a verbal report from me of the occasion of my absence, which I subsequently made in writing, I had the extreme gratification of being again thanked by him for the protection of the sick and wounded, and baggage under my care. There is pleasure in serving such a General, ever ready courteously to acknowledge a service.

After a short rest, I was once more in the saddle, and galloped back to the scene of our recent fight, to ascertain what had become of two guns that we had spiked. On my return, I found the entire force in motion towards Busserat Gunge, following the direct road. I put spurs to my horse, which had unfortunately lost a shoe and got lame, so that its speed little accorded with my impatience. At this town we met with much more determined opposition than at the former. It is walled, and is surrounded with wet ditches; a round tower defends the gates, five guns being on and near it, while a loop-holed building in close proximity adds to its strength. A water-cut of some depth, and of no inconsiderable breadth, lies to the rear of the town; this is approached by a narrow causeway, from which a bridge is thrown across.

The enemy opened a brisk cannonade upon us as the guns pushed on in their usual fine order, supported by Madras Fusiliers, skirmishing, and 78th Highlanders and 64th, in line. Notwithstanding the severity of their fire, we continued to gain ground. The 64th were ordered to turn the town, get between it and the bridge, and cut off the enemy from the causeway and bridge; panting for victory, the Fusiliers and Highlanders flung themselves upon the earthworks, broke into the entrenchments, and captured the town.

Cavalry was utterly useless, it being quite impossible for them to act, from the flooded state of the roads. Still, we took a quantity of ammunition, and a large number of guns. By sunset we were in possession of the town. Lieutenant Havelock, Her Majesty's 10th, brave as his sire, had a horse shot under him; and Lieutenant Macpherson, Adjutant of the 78th, was conspicuous for daring.

Our ranks, since crossing the river, the day's casualties included, are now reduced to eleven hundred Europeans; our ambulance is exhausted; every *palanquin* and *dhoolie* for carrying sick and wounded occupied. Lucknow, to reach which is our anxious desire, is thirty miles distant.

After the battle of Busserat Gunge, our general passed down the narrow street, thronged with wearied soldiers. They, on observing him, cried out: "Clear the way for the General!"

To this he instantly made answer: "You have done that well already."

Never was compliment more happily timed, or more warmly appreciated; they were literally transported with delight, praise being the soldier's coveted reward and best stimulant. Despite his reserved manner, no man is more capable of conciliating, I had almost said compelling, regard than General Havelock.

July 30th

We are within thirty miles of Lucknow, where our compatriots are beset by our implacable enemy, and yet are unable to succour them. Our little band is decimated by disease, the cruel foes, dysentery and cholera, thinning our reduced ranks, while the reeking pestilential atmosphere, incident to swampy ground, engenders those disorders.

Today we are to fall back upon Mungurwar, an order which, though emanating from such wise foresight as merits applause, is yet most unwelcome to those bold, eager spirits, burning for fresh enterprise and panting to relieve our countrymen. The very idea of a retrograde movement filled them with consternation; its present reality calls forth the first murmurs I have yet heard.

A man of less genuine mettle than our General might be swayed by such demonstrations, but the superiority of his moral courage renders him unassailable, and elevates him far beyond the fear of man, which bringeth a snare.

Prudence, as well as courage, is one of the first virtues of a soldier, a duty to be sedulously cultivated; so much depending on its exercise, and so many human lives. Nor is any act or decision of our leaders more to be lauded than this. To risk a further reduction of our numbers now would be culpable rashness, the more especially as we expect reinforcements shortly.

And yet such is man, when he fixes his desires upon one object, that the predominant and almost universal feeling in our little band is one of indignation at not being led forward.

In compliance with General Havelock's request, I am henceforth to act as his *aid-de-camp*, vice Seton, a most promising young officer. Poor fellow! The suffering, consequent upon the wound he received through the face, is excessively acute.

This day is marked by the execution of some fugitive Sepoys; two of them were blown from a gun. The fortitude with which they met this punishment was remarkable, and worthy of a better cause. They were both extremely fine men, in the flower of their age—tall, athletic, graceful, with finely-moulded limbs, almost resembling antique statues in bronze.

The first approached the engine of destruction with an unwavering, firm tread, his head erect and eye fearless; undauntedly, almost contemptuously, he gazed around while he was being secured to the muzzle of the gun.

No sooner was the word "fire" given, than the discharge ensued, with a peculiar muffled report, which rent his body to atoms, while a sickening effluvium tainted the atmosphere as his head was flung aloft far into the blue aether.

From the spreading branches of an adjacent tree, two wretches who had suffered death by hanging were dangling.

July 31st

Yesterday afternoon we fell back to Oonao, where we halted, and were glad of the shelter of native huts and trees, but I was in no very agreeable mood. Though my evening meal was a scanty one, yet it sufficed, and the prospect of repose was most welcome to me.

The small tent that constitutes my office is a little impromptu hospital, at present being occupied by Lieutenant Boyle, 78th, wounded severely in the action of the 29th, and Captain Maycock, 53rd, Deputy Assistant Quartermaster General, sick from the effects of immersion whilst ascertaining the depth of a sheet of water in front of the enemy's right flank, for the information of the General.

We are now again upon our former camping ground at Mungurwar, having continued our march from Oonao towards the left bank of the Ganges. My shoulder, chest and side have been again very troublesome—the pain, at times, excruciating; but, fortunately, they do not prevent the fulfilment of my duties.

CHAPTER 8

Bithoor

An attack of dysentery at Mungurwar weakened me so much that, despite every effort of my will, I became prostrated to such a degree as to be utterly incapable of further exertion, and was reluctantly compelled to re-cross to this place, with the sick and wounded, on the first opportunity that presented itself. To this measure I was in some degree reconciled by the hope of being able to get on from hence to Delhi, my regiment being in front of it; for to share with my old comrades in the dangers of the siege is my anxious desire. The news we received of the fall of that place was premature, and it now appears that the mutineers are making a stout resistance and giving us more trouble than was anticipated. However, the self-reliance of British soldiers on their own martial prowess is truly wonderful, and one of the surest elements of success.

AUGUST 15TH

Our intrepid general, on hearing about two days ago (Thursday last) of the enemy having again occupied Busserat Gunge (fourteen miles in advance), from whence we had only a few days previously compelled him to fly, determined once more to force him to abandon his position, despite the formidable array of his replenished ranks, amounting now to four thousand men, together with six field-guns. They had entrenched themselves in the village of Boorbie Ackeckowkie, in advance of Busserat

Gunge, their front being protected by wide and deep morasses, across which it seemed impossible for us to move the batteries necessary for the attack. Our troops suffered heavily in crossing the swamp, being exposed to the fire of the enemy's artillery posted in front; but the indomitable courage which had borne them through so many contests throbbed with still fuller life in each warrior-heart, and bore them on to victory. Uttering a loud cheer of mingled assurance and defiance, the brave Highlanders, without the expenditure of a single shot, flung themselves impetuously on the principal redoubt, defended by three horse-battery guns, two of which they captured. The Madras Fusiliers, meantime, put the enemy's extreme left completely to the rout, and soon his entire line was driven to retreat.

This was the eighth engagement since the 12th of July! In all of these, our arms had triumphed, notwithstanding every advantage being on the side of our adversaries!

This well-timed movement of our General's, carried out, as it was, in so masterly a manner, has been of the utmost importance, as he has been enabled thereby to re-cross the Ganges. Our troops, however, were severely tried; the advance into Cawnpore seemed as much as it was possible for men to endure, and the excessive heat proved fatal to many during the march. But what we then endured was comparatively light, in comparison with what we encountered while advancing into Oude, and again in returning hither. Such has been the effect that many in our ranks, who, on leaving Allahabad were robust and healthy, are now worn and emaciated. We now buoy ourselves up with the hope of fresh troops from England, but even if despatched overland, as we are led to expect, two full months must elapse before it is possible for them to arrive here.

Threatened as we are on every side, will our little handful of men, which is too likely to be reduced in number still further by sunstroke and disease—shall we be able to struggle on during that time? This place seems hardly tenable, yet the feebleness of the defensive works of Cawnpore is perhaps compensated by the noble spirit of our troops; for every soldier seems to vie with another in the zealous performance of duty. No cases of malingering exist; even those who are really ill are unwilling to admit their illness.

Though I was obliged to return here on the sixth of this month, weakened by dysentery, yet, on the ninth, I was again under orders to accompany a force at a moment's notice, to meet and engage a body of mutineers who have been hovering about us for some days.

To enable us to meet such contingencies, our numbers can ill-afford reduction, yet cholera and dysentery are at present fearfully on the increase. Great anxiety is expressed by our highly-efficient medical officers, in consequence of the rapid progress of these diseases. The extraordinary exposure, how-ever, to which our troops have been subject at a season of the year, which, on account of its many vicissitudes, is very trying to Europeans, would naturally predispose the soldiers to cholera and dysentery, even if they had received either the poor shelter of a tent, or the comfort of a bed, whereon to rest after a weary march. From these comparative luxuries they parted when they crossed the Ganges into Oude. Onward they marched—unshrinking, whether tortured by the scorching sun, or chilled by the heavy rain, or almost suffocated by the atmosphere, pregnant with electricity, and reeking with foetid exhalations from the swampy ground. All this time, the scanty supply of indifferent food afforded but poor nutriment, and was ill-adapted to repair that waste of bodily strength, which might have enabled them to resist disease. Even the air which we now breathe is instinct with animal life.

Here the entomologist would now find every variety of fly and winged creature, both sightly and unsightly. Here reptiles super-abound, vermin frisk about unmolested, and multitudes of Jackals disturb our broken rest at night, as they prowl over the station, uttering doleful cries like the voice of human wailing.

Brigadier-General Neil is now in command of the canton-ment; and, as at Benares and Allahabad, his presence has already exercised a beneficial influence. Under his wise supervision, order is gradually emerging out of chaos. Every morning at day-break, he makes a circuit of the town, to reassure the shopkeep-ers, who are oft affrighted by rumours of the rebels approaching in overwhelming numbers to attack the station, which from its, extent is scarcely tenable.

Meanwhile, the troops destined to reinforce us are detained, *en route* from Calcutta, at other stations, where the spirit of disaf-fection is paramount.

We are now quartered in such houses as have escaped the fury of the mutineers. They are situated upon the river side, and though they have more or less suffered, are a welcome change from the native huts.

Here also our hospital-tents are pitched, and they are full to overflowing. These are covered by a field-work. Fortunately for our men, the cavalry stable-sheds still remain standing. These serve them for quarters, no barrack room being in existence, and the inundated state of the plain rendering it quite unfit for an encampment.

In the native town, many rebels and mutineers have been discovered in different lurking-places. They have been sentenced to death by hanging, but before suffering this extreme penalty, have been compelled by the Brigadier to wipe up the blood of our martyred country-women from the floor of the house where they were sacrificed. Close to this house, the gallows is erected. The original mind of the Brigadier suggested this novel mode of punishment, which is utterly antagonistic to the preju-dices of the people, and is attended with the forfeiture of caste. Strange inconsistency! These very people, who believe, or affect to believe, that the penalty of everlasting perdition is entailed by forfeiting the privilege of caste, can resistlessly submit to it while unable by it to escape death.

BIVOUAC, BITHOOR, AUGUST 17TH

Yesterday (Sunday) I accompanied the force under General Havelock to this place, nine miles distant from Cawnpore. Mu-tineers from Saugor, Fyzabad, and other stations, have joined a number of Nana Sahib's troops, in all about four thousand, and occupied Bithoor, one of the strongest positions in India. The plain, being overgrown with thick sugar-cane and stunted trees, affords ample cover to the enemy.

It has villages on either flank, and is intersected by two rapid streams, impossible to ford, and only to be crossed by insignificant bridges, the most distant of which is defended by an entrenchment protected by artillery.

When this latter bridge is traversed, the road curves in such a manner as to shelter the defenders from direct fire, and beyond, in the rear, are the narrow streets and brick houses of Bithoor. But notwithstanding the many advantages of his position, the enemy as usual succumbed, being unable to resist even the small force we brought into the field. The original strength of the 78th, which I accompanied on foot, had been 284 rank and file; it was now miserably reduced. Still it was animated by the same fine spirit as had always characterised it.

A strong body of the mutineer's cavalry, having appeared in our front to reconnoitre, was saluted by a few rounds from our artillery. At the sound of the discharge, all our men seemed inspired with renewed energy, which became keener still as we discovered the position taken up by the enemy, its centre resting on a bridge flanked by an entrenched battery, which commanded the centre of our line of advance. Both his flanks were well covered by plantation. Behind lay the town of Bithoor, thickly studded with brick houses, rising one above another, surrounded by walls, and buried in trees. No pause ensued. The Madras Fusiliers, followed by the Artillery, under Captain Crump, took up position on the plain, and the 78th Highlanders completed the right centre, on one side of the road. Our left wing, 64th, 84th, and Sikh regiment of Ferozepore, with Olpherts' battery, prolonged the line to the left, on the other side of the road.

Soon, our right was found to be enfiladed by matchlockmen, posted in a village partly masked by trees; but this was speedily met by throwing back the right companies of the Madras Fusiliers, who had the honour of carrying the village.

On our leaving the road, the enemy's guns opened fire upon us with much precision, directing their fire upon our right centre, consisting of the 78th Highlanders. We evaded it by lying down at intervals, as our guns halted to answer his fire. All this continued till we were within four hundred yards of his position. We were then assailed by a well-directed rifle-fire, which was briskly answered from our right by the Madras Fusiliers, who poured a withering volley upon the enemy from a long range, and followed up their volley by an admirable advance in line.

To keep pace longer with the tardy advance of our bullock-battery, was a work too tedious for the impatience of our troops. The 78th accordingly sprung forward and seized the battery in front, while the enemy sullenly abandoned his position. Our toil-worn soldiers were too much exhausted to pursue, but many of the mutineers, greatly fatigued, fell down beneath our bayonets.

I had never before seen so close and well-directed a fire of small arms.

A considerable number of the mutineers had posted themselves in a square redoubt earthwork, from which their riflemen fired upon our right wing, and with much effect. Their position was concealed, till the Highlanders, led on by Lieutenant Cassidy of the light company, advanced within a hundred yards and pushed them out of it. Our right battalion, the Madras Fusiliers, led the charge, giving simultaneously a long and thrilling cheer. In this advance our right wing was chiefly engaged, while Captain Olpherts, always conspicuous for daring, conducted his battery far in advance of our left centre. His intention, I believe, was to take the enemy's line, had not orders to prevent him meantime been issued. We here advanced, upon the heels of the mutineers, to the bridge adjacent to the road before described.

The leading officer, Lieutenant Cassidy, was in eager pursuit of a mounted *sowar*, whom he might have made prisoner, had not the halt been sounded to enable the left wing to join us, which was soon effected. He also took the lead in pursuing the enemy through a long street, flanked on our right with garden enclosures. Under the cover of these enclosures, the foe kept up a biting fire. Several of our men, completely wayworn, sank down exhausted on the road side, where they lay powerless; others again, endued either with greater physical strength or more determined volition, displayed increased resolution to silence the fire of our adversaries. We could stand this no longer, but charged at three hundred yards, when the enemy left the position, retiring slowly, and seemingly quite as much fatigued as ourselves. A large enclosure surrounding the Residency, originally occupied by the British agent near the Nana, afforded a welcome halting place to the over tasked troops, who lay down to rest beneath the shade of umbrageous trees. Short, however, was the respite, for they were quickly warned to "go on," as it was necessary to clear the town.

It being exceedingly intricate, there was much trouble in dislodging the enemy from it, nor was it effected without severe fighting in the barricaded houses.

A Highlander, and one of the Madras Fusiliers, possessed of but one rifle between them, in the heat of excitement, rushed into one of these houses, where they discovered seven Sepoys. Not one of the seven escaped; they all were victims to the avenging spirit of those two Europeans, who proudly related the adventure.

At one time, our general had determined to follow the enemy to Soorajpore, but, being destitute of cavalry, abandoned the intention. This afternoon, a great many of our men sickened.

We had brought no tents with us, and therefore lay down to sleep beneath the trees, happy in possessing such a shelter. At Bithoor, as well as at Cawnpore, the mutineers exhibited the strongest symptoms of vexation after suffering themselves to be beaten by numbers so inferior. They smashed their muskets in their rage, upbraiding themselves upon their defeat, and, like true Asiatics, "weeping like women for what they could not hold like men."

Having blown up the buildings, the property of the Nana at Bithoor, we returned to Cawnpore, and in passing the position from whence we had driven the mutineers, we became aware of the superior advantages of defence which it afforded, being screened from observation by a thick plantation of maples, closely occupied by their infantry, and immediately in rear of a gun-battery, which for nearly a mile commanded our approach. Our troops were much exposed to the fire of this battery, as they quitted the main road and moved across the position in order to make a direct attack.

Never can I forget the daring manner in which Olpherts, with his battery of horse artillery, menaced one point of their position, or the gallantry of McPherson of the 78th, ever cheering on his men in front of the line. Our number of sick is lamentably augmented by this one day's work at Bithoor, where many have been also disabled by wounds, some killed, and others have died of sunstroke or cholera.

It was really piteous to see our fine fellows lying disabled in the large enclosed garden of the Residency. Our doctors are quite overworked, for the cases of acute dysentery are painfully numerous, and generally terminate in cholera. There is no greater predisposing cause to illness of this kind than long fasting, especially in a country like this, where the bodily waste is so rapid. As it is desirable to repair this waste, the greatest care should be taken, when possible, to prevent men from having to undergo the pangs of hunger as well as the languor of fatigue, and therefore the department which supplies their food should be well superintended. By certain precautions on this head, there is little doubt that much sickness might be avoided.

The lesson given by General Havelock to the rebels, on the 16th, will, I think, effectually prevent them from showing themselves in his vicinity for some time to come.

CHAPTER 9

The British Soldier

AUGUST 22ND

In the absence of positive intelligence from our beleaguered countrymen at Lucknow, our anxiety about them is supreme. We scarcely dare to indulge the hope that the garrison are continuing to hold out, and we live on from day to day in expectation of learning some fatal news. Sir Hugh Wheeler was the last to afford them relief, by sending detachments of Her Majesty's 32nd and 84th to Lucknow, heedless of his own critical position, and with strange infatuation relying on the fidelity of the native troops under his command. These troops, as is now credibly reported, made their intended mutiny the subject of their daily discussion, without any attempt at concealment. Hints were given both to the civil and military authorities here, but it does not appear that they took any notice of the warning.

It may have been that the hapless Sir Hugh Wheeler, a well-worn veteran, with his characteristic frank-heartedness, relied too implicitly on the hope of promised assistance reaching him by the 15th of June, which appears to be attested, if what I have heard be true, by official documents since discovered.

The part played by the Nana in this foul tragedy was worthy the genius of an Asiatic, marked by craft, dissimulation, and treachery. He proffered his services as a friend to take over the magazine. Such was the reliance placed on his fidelity, that not only the magazine was given into his protection, but the treasury was also placed under his charge. Having thus pared the lion's claws, our countrymen no longer made it his policy to dissimulate. He became their open foe, till it again suited the purposes of the arch-traitor to resume the mask, and to hasten on the appalling crisis, by pledging himself, by all that he held most sacred, to observe the proposed treaty inviolate; which expressly stipulated the unmolested departure of the British in boats down the Ganges.

Yet, simultaneously, with fiendish perfidiousness, he notified to the native officer in command on the banks of the river, that they were about to embark, and laid a strict injunction upon this subordinate not to suffer them to proceed to any distance, remarking in his official letter, found in his order book:

> The Ferringhees say (or think) they are going down to Calcutta, but you will do your duty as becomes a faithful servant.

Poor young Glanville, 2nd Bengal Fusiliers, with whom I had been a fellow-passenger from England but a month previously, and whom I sedulously endeavoured to accompany to Cawnpore, when proceeding thence from Calcutta, was killed in one of the ill-fated boats.

But to return to our force. Cholera is now more than ever busy amongst us, and four of our Volunteer Horse have been buried today. Poor Brown has also fallen a victim to this deadly malady, which, from foregone exposure and privation, he had not stamina sufficient to resist. He was one of those who had escaped the massacre ordered by the execrable Nana in the boats, but his sufferings were extraordinary.

Utterly destitute of clothing, he arrived in our camp, worn to a shadow, and much embrowned by exposure. His entire bearing was wild and haggard. For six weeks, he had been swimming along the Ganges, tortured by the flaming sunshine, gnawed by hunger, wearied by sustained exertion, bereft almost of hope, destitute, afflicted, tormented. In peril often, he now and then obtained from compassionate natives, who were not afraid to assist him, a little food, till, at length, he reached our camp; but, after escaping death in so many other forms, succumbed to cholera.

The atrocities we hear of are manifold. An unfortunate lady, resident here, was, with her five children, confided by her husband (who belonged to the garrison) to the care of a native servant, on whose fidelity they both placed the most implicit reliance. He swore, indeed, to defend them to the death. During his absence on some errand, the house they occupied was attacked by the mutineers. They, however, made their escape, and succeeded in concealing themselves amongst some bushes.

The servant returned, leant what had occurred, went in search of the unhappy fugitives, whom he had solemnly sworn to protect, and killed them all himself.

This has been the happiest day I have known for many weeks, as the post has brought me letters from my wife and child, which have been as cold waters to the thirsty soul.

30TH AUGUST

We are still at Cawnpore, while our enemies on the opposite bank are busily engaged throwing obstacles in the way of our second advance to relieve Lucknow. It is painful to know that when last we heard, which is about three or four days since, the besieged had no prospect of being able to hold out longer than ten days. What will their fate be? A repetition of the fearful Cawnpore tragedy? Dreary idea! There are fifty ladies, with their families, in that doomed city. Oh, that England could know the peril of her children!

No available force is there to rescue those hapless creatures, save our miserable band, strong only in its bravery. Numerous and fierce hordes have we to strive against unaided; nor does it seem to us probable that reinforcements can reach us before the 1st of December, now that we have learnt they are to be sent round the Cape.

Were next month past, matters would assume a more hopeful prospect; but all events are controlled by an Almighty power, in whose good providence it behoves us to trust.

The advance of the Gwalior rebels, a numerous and well organised body, to attack Cawnpore, is now confidently rumoured; and to repel them we must make preparation.

Cholera still rages amongst us. A brave officer of Her Majesty's 81st Regiment has been carried off in a few hours by this malady. Though only eight years in the army, he had served with distinction as a volunteer in the Crimean War down to the fall of Sevastopol. He had volunteered to come up here from Persia with our force, being every inch a soldier. Irish by birth, he had a ready wit and a most engaging frankness of manner. He was also an excellent companion. He was beloved by all his brother volunteers, who anxiously watched the progress of his disease, and ministered to his wants with tender solicitude. Their attentions, however, were ineffectual—his slight frame bowed to the destroyer, incapable of resistance. He has left a name above all blight of earthly breath—a memory of which his friends may be proud—that of an upright, honourable man.

With the hope of diverting the minds of our troops from dwelling too much upon the fatal influences by which they are surrounded, games have been set on foot for their amusement, with music in the afternoon; but what has interested them more than anything else, is the arrival of a family which has been saved by the intervention of a friendly native. The appearance of the solitary lady by whom the fugitives have been accompanied, is a stimulant to the curiosity of the men, who had been now for months without seeing a European woman, and are ever anxiously on the watch for a glimpse of the new arrival. They may be seen in knots of from four to five, discussing the probable adventures and escapes which she has met with in her wanderings, and praising the good feeling of her native preserver.

Fine fellows they are! And most truly are their hearts open to the influence of melting charity! Lips that have breathed the firmest imprecations of vengeance against the destroyers, whose ruthless hearts quenched their lust for slaughter in the blood of gentle women and innocent babes, now fashion the softest expressions of sympathy.

The close band of union which exists between our men is the secret of our strength. They err, who look down upon the British soldier and consider him one of a degraded class. Could they but see those noble-hearted men amongst whom I live, they would recognise them as fearless, enduring, and contented. The very hardships and privations, which they have had to encounter, seem to have developed latent qualities of excellence, that exalt humanity, and elevate the man above the beasts that perish.

And what has England done for her soldier sons?—For those men whose profession exposes them to every imaginable peril, and on whom she relies for protection? Has she treated them as sons?—Has she extended the robe of civilisation to them, as to her other children, with maternal love, considering for their health of body, of mind, and of morals? Or has hers been the part of a cruel step-mother, to whom their well-being is a matter of perfect indifference? Does she look upon them as mere hirelings, of whom the most is to be made? And does she consider that, in paying them their wages, she has fulfilled her contract? Has she treated them as sons?

Let the barrack accommodation which she has provided for them, and let the annual bills of mortality among them, answer that question.

Has she extended the robe of civilisation to them? Let the abomination of the barrack-room, common to both sexes, determine.

For her other children, she has liberally provided baths and wash-houses, built model lodging-houses, and sought to keep decency intact. Can she regard her soldier sons as men of the like passions with other creatures of sense and appetite? Or does she suppose, because their reason is not cultivated, invention stimulated, or intellectual power developed, they are the better able to control powerful inclination? To the rudest savages, the honour of their women is dear, not less so (even all exposed as it is) to the British soldier.

I could adduce more than one tragic incident in support of this, when the infuriated husband has poured out the lifeblood of his wife to wash away her pollution.

Fathers and husbands in high places, by whom female purity is esteemed and cherished, how long will ye abstain from raising your voices in reprobation of a system so subversive of morality as that which at present exists?

It is a blot on the fair fame of your beloved England—a reproach to any nation.

The welfare of the soldier has always been most dear to me, and from the noble examples I have lately witnessed in the ranks of those fine regiments with which I serve in this force, it has become more than ever a matter of interest. Their cheerfulness amid unparalleled suffering, their dauntless courage in the hour of danger, their ready submission to the iron rule of adverse circumstances, all prove the stuff of which they are made, and their capabilities of further improvement.

To make good soldiers, good officers are necessary; officers who consider the service, not a pastime to idle away a few years of their life, but as a profession to be practically acquired, and to be studied as assiduously as any of those yclept learned. To a person who considers the duties which it involves, the responsibility is great, and the requirements many; amongst which latter may be ranked, knowledge of human nature, self-respect, temperance in all things, forbearance, and firmness. Endued with such qualities, none of which are beyond the reach of those who desire to attain them, a man soon gains the esteem of his subordinates, and secures their confidence. In a regiment, generally, the conduct of its several companies illustrates the character of its officers, and very probably, if that were made the test of promotion, there would be a marked improvement in our army.

Chapter 10

Lucknow Reached

SEPTEMBER 1ST

This is the birthday of my son, and such is a soldier's life, while he is far away in peaceful England, here I am, surrounded by the rude havoc of war, fallen houses, perforated with shot, and by many other indications of strife, past, present, and to come.

Meanwhile, preparations are being made, under the supervision of the indefatigable Captain Crommelin, for crossing the Ganges, by a bridge of boats, into Oude, while; on the opposite bank, the enemy are busily engaged in making obstructions to our progress.

Detachments of the 78th, 64th, and 84th have arrived. Moreover, Her Majesty's 5th and 70th, recalled from the China expedition, with Sir James Outram, a tried and valued servant of the Honourable Company, are already at Allahabad, *en route* hither, where their arrival is eagerly expected. As soon as we are reinforced, and arrangements are completed for crossing the Ganges, we proceed once more to the relief of the heroic Lucknow garrison, of which we have again received intelligence; but it is so conflicting, that there is difficulty in unravelling the truth.

Illness still lingers among us, and cholera is frequent. There cannot be a sorer scourge to humanity than this ruthless malady, which seems to baffle all efforts of medical science.

From what I have observed, it appears that persons of desponding temperament are more exposed to its influence than those of a buoyant mind. It is, however, no easy matter to resist depression amid general gloom, but a strong, determined will effects wonders.

My servant, for I have at last acquired the comfort of having a servant, manifests great concern about my health, and, although he is a Mahommedan, shows marks of personal attachment. The prejudice against all this caste is at present naturally strong, but justice compels me to notice his seeming good qualities.

September 3rd

There is no abatement in the heavy rain, or in the insect swarm.

In the evening, when our lamps are lit, they are a perfect torment. I have seen one very curious kind, which, I have been told, persons of Epicurean tastes consider a great delicacy, but though they were presented to me on a fresh green leaf, with a spoon to eat them, by my servant, yet, I confess, I had not sufficient enthusiasm in gastronomic research to yield to the temptation. I was, however, in the act of raising some three or four to my lips to taste them, when I observed them in motion. Till then, I believed them to be some sort of fruit or berry. They are of a rich carnation colour, and of soft velvet-like appearance, with that peculiar bloom noticeable on raspberries freshly ripened. They are about the size of a ladybird, but sounder and plumper, and are altogether a very pretty specimen of insect life. I am too ignorant of entomology to be able to determine their species, farther than to maintain that they are not the cochineal. My servant was greatly disappointed at the repulsion I manifested. He assured me that they were deemed an especial dainty, were greatly esteemed by the wealthy natives, and were an object of much competition that day in the *bazaar*, but he was determined that his Sahib, and no other, should have them.

Notwithstanding all these arguments in favour of eating them, my prejudice was not to be overcome.

The heat of the atmosphere is very trying and oppressive, close and sultry, and charged with electricity.

There are times when an irresistible feeling of enervation

possesses me, so that I can neither read, write, nor think, but lapse into a vague dreamy mood. This is generally disturbed by a shrill, peculiar cry, emitted by a lizard, when lo! a whole troop of those reptiles disport themselves on walls and ceiling, some of them pretty creatures of vivid green, burnished with orange, and others of a pale, loathsome, tawny colour. We are all weary of this inactivity, and desire once more to resume our march. We hope within a few days to have our reinforcement, and then again to proceed to the relief of the heroic Garrison at Lucknow.

SEPTEMBER 18TH

The welcome order to resume our march is issued, and immediately after day-break tomorrow, our present life of inaction will be exchanged for one of excitement.

Difficulties, hardships, and dangers we must encounter, but this gloomy prospect is more than counterbalanced by the hope of being able to effect the deliverance of our gallant countrymen from their durance at Lucknow. Indeed, I firmly believe that there is not a single individual of the entire force, now greatly augmented, who does not rejoice in the prospect, if not of liberating them, at least of making the attempt. The noble endurance and the unshaken fortitude of that brave garrison will be handed down to posterity in historic record, as an example worthy alike of wonder and admiration.

The rebels are still to be seen on the opposite side, busily engaged in making preparations to resist our advance into Oude; but the spirit which animates our force makes light of difficulties. To do, to dare, to die, if it may be so, but still to overcome, is its determination. Today the enemy had the insolence to open fire upon our picquets, sent to hold the landing-place. It was but slight, and of short duration, as if they feared to rouse the sleeping lion. The peculiarly long and tangled grass, which grows in profusion upon the banks, affords them ample cover for numbers, and facilitates their power of annoying us.

I intend to bring my *palanquin* carriage with me, as it may be useful to convey some helpless sufferer from Lucknow. Meantime it will be of use to me upon the march, for I intend it to do duty as my bed, and also as my office to read or write in when we halt; so that I shall feel quite as independent as the philosophic cobbler—

Who lived in a stall,
That served him as a parlour, kitchen, and hall.

The predominant feeling now is one of enthusiastic admiration of the magnanimity displayed by Sir James Outram, in relinquishing his own just claim to command the force, in favour of General Havelock. Such self-abnegation is as admirable as it is rare, and could emanate only from a mind superior to envy and all petty feeling of rivalry. No action of his life betokens more greatness, than this chivalrous act of self-forgetfulness, which practically illustrates the Christian principle of doing unto others as we would be ourselves done by. There will be no brighter page in the history of the great Indian rebellion of 1857, than that which will record this noble recognition of General Havelock's exertions, this just appreciation of his merits. There is something absolutely grand in the very simplicity, which marks the following order of Sir James Outram.

> It would be unfair of me to assume the command, after all the efforts made by General Havelock to reach Lucknow, for whom the honour of relieving its beleaguered garrison is reserved.

With two such leaders, and troops like ours, it is hard if we do not achieve our aim.

September 21st

A little after dawn, on the 19th, we recommenced our march into the enemy's country, which we succeeded in reaching; part of the troops having crossed the bridge of boats, thrown across the Ganges by Captain Crommelin, whose energy and indefatigable perseverance are an incitement to his staff and subordinates, and beyond all praise. This bridge was covered by our twenty-four pounders, and a *tête-de-pont*, planned by young Moorsom of

Her Majesty's 52nd, an officer of extraordinary promise. His capabilities on a campaign seem inexhaustible, and emanate from a military genius of no common order.

When our Generals, Sir James Outram and the dauntless Havelock, proceeded to cross the river, some trifling opposition was offered by the enemy from the shelter of a ridge of sand-hills.

This was met by our skirmishers with their usual spirit, especially Her Majesty's 5th Fusiliers, lately arrived from Mauritius, who displayed the most perfect training.

The accuracy of their fire was such as to produce evident symptoms of discomfiture amongst the enemy, who speedily abandoned his post, ceased to defend himself, and retreated with the guns which he had brought up, falling back upon the village of Mungurwar, about two miles distant in front.

On nearing Mungurwar, we saw the enemy again posted on the plain commanding our line of route, his left resting on a village which afforded great cover, from the luxuriant growth of standing com that rose before it as a screen, while a drizzling rain enveloped it in haze.

We moved forward from the road in oblique line for the purpose of turning the right flank of the insurgents, whose batteries had meantime opened, and were directed chiefly upon our heavy guns drawn by elephants, killing some of the detachment escorting them.

The sagacious animals displayed their usual caution, at once turning back, and could not be induced to drag on the guns, to which bullocks were then attached, to obviate this difficulty. Beyond this our line experienced but little resistance, and sweeping onward, with the 90th Light Infantry on its left, in dashing style, soon cleared the plantation and village; the hasty retreat of the rebels being simultaneous with our advance. Now, for the first time, a fair opportunity was opened to the gallant Barrow, who, during our halt at Cawnpore, had been indefatigable in training and disciplining his Volunteer Horse, which he led in the pursuit, accompanied by Sir James Outram.

In this pursuit a heavy gun was taken, and numbers of the fugitives were cut up; but Sir James Outram, disdaining to use a sword with such recreants, charged them with a heavy cudgel, which he used with considerable effect upon the bodies of the runaways. The loss on our side in this affair was very trifling, a fortunate circumstance, as we can ill spare even one—the total strength of our force, augmented as it now is, not amounting to quite three thousand.

While this action continued, the rain, which had only been a slight mist in the commencement of it, fell in torrents, darkening the atmosphere, obscuring our view, and rendering our footing doubly insecure on the swampy ground.

Our Commissariat and stores had been safely brought across.

Baggage we had none, all that being left behind at Cawnpore, from whence we set out to undertake this expedition in light marching order. I wonder when we shall know the luxury of a dry jacket. Under existing circumstances, a faith in the cold-water system would be, doubtless, very consolatory.

Our column of route re-formed, and marched to Busserrat Gunge, fourteen miles from Cawnpore, which we occupied for the night.

Yesterday, for the first time since I joined this force, I saw General Havelock without his military frock. This was occasioned by his hurry to discover the cause of a most absurd panic which prevailed amongst our camp followers, who came pouring into camp from our right rear, driving in elephants, camels, &c., with the utmost confusion and dismay. In a moment, however, the general had resumed his accustomed dress, which he put on outside his tent, was quickly in his saddle, and was seen riding to the rear, where he discovered that the alarm was a false one.

SEPTEMBER 22ND

We marched upon Bunee, through incessant rain. The route, however, was quite clear. At three o'clock, p.m., we crossed the bridge, on either side of which were deserted stockaded batteries.

Our progress was now expeditious, as the falling rain had cooled the air, and enabled us to march more easily. Our force halted along the road, a mile in front of the bridge, where, during the afternoon, we fired a royal salute, in the hope that its report would reach the beleaguered garrison at Lucknow, and be received by them as an intimation of our approach.

Although we doubted the probability that it would reach so far, yet it was not impossible, and our anxious wish was to make them aware of coming aid.

During the night, many armed natives succeeded in concealing themselves in the village, from whence they contrived to escape, and afterwards to waylay our Dak, which they robbed.

I found some railway-wire bullets and powder in the village. These I gave over to General Havelock.

Next day we continued to march towards Lucknow, having set out at eight, a.m. It was quite a contrast to the preceding day, for the atmosphere was so close and oppressive as to be almost stifling. At half-past two, p.m., we made a reconnaissance, when the cavalry discovered the enemy three miles in front, occupying three mounds: their left resting on the main road. So well had the enemy chosen his position, that it is a matter of astonishment he did not maintain it, the more especially as our movement was not planned judiciously. An expanse of water, which lay on the enemy's left, obstructed the advance of our column.

We had, therefore, to sweep past as best we could, in order to front the enemy, close upon his batteries, to which we were unnecessarily exposed, but from which he might, almost to a certainty, have been dislodged by some companies of the Enfield riflemen.

The distance of range was within eight hundred yards, and easy to be attained by that invaluable weapon, the Enfield rifle, the capabilities of which have been too often overlooked or neglected, and never sufficiently tested. Had our 5th Fusiliers been permitted the opportunity of using them on this occasion across the sheet of water, not a few saddles of the rebel cavalry would have been emptied, while the batteries opposed to us would have been made untenable from our bullets. Thus, much bloodshed and loss of life would have been spared in our ranks, for there was neither cover nor support from our guns, while we deployed into line; an imprudent move, by which the paucity of our troops was too plainly revealed.

A desire to ascertain our numbers might probably have caused the enemy to take up this position, along the whole front of which we had to pass, regiment by regiment.

Her Majesty's 5th Fusiliers, which passed first, suffered severely. The adjutant, Lieutenant Haig, and several men, were killed by round shot from the enemy; while, strange to observe, his numerous cavalry, though within a few hundred yards, and facing our line of march along the road, suffered us to pass unmolested.

Our right front was much annoyed from the Alum Bagh, where the enemy poured a smart fire upon us; but he was speedily driven from thence, and retired upon the city. He was pursued some distance by the Volunteer Horse, led by Sir James Outram, towards the city bridge. Char Bagh. This advance was supported by a battery of two regiments; but it was resolved to defer the final one till the next day. As yet we have -had no communication from the beleaguered garrison at Lucknow, ardently as we have hoped for it; but we had many misgivings about their fate before we left Cawnpore. However, during the night of the 23rd, much firing was heard from the direction of the city.

September 24th

From an early hour this mornings cavalry might be observed from the position occupied by our baggage, stealing along singly and cautiously to a village not far from where our carts are stationed.

This was duly reported; a request also was preferred that a gun might be ordered to strengthen our rear-guard. Unfortunately this was not attended to, and the men on duty, unsuspicious of danger, straggled away from the post of alarm, with the exception of a few who remained on the alert. At length the cavalry, which had been so long hovering in the distance, like a bird of prey watching its victim, dashed suddenly on the road, accompanied by a body of Sepoys, making much noise and shouting vociferously. This so terrified the drivers and other camp followers, that they hastily fled, abandoning the baggage. So simultaneous was their flight, and so rapid, that it resembled the sound of a rushing storm sweeping over the plain, which was scattered with numerous unclad, dusky forms, like figures of animated bronze. Fortunately for me, as the event proved, I had, on the previous evening, moved my palanquin carriage nearer to our lines than the position which it had occupied amongst the baggage.

Only a few minutes before this onslaught, I had been indulging in such a bath as was attainable, and which greatly partook of the character of a mud one, the water being taken from the roadside, where it had lodged after the ram.

My servant poured it over me as I sat luxuriating in this attempt at ablution, the first I had had for some days, in front of the space occupied by my palanquin carriage. Luckily I was dressed in time to have returned, when this attack was made; otherwise I could never have escaped. For some minutes the confusion was extreme, and *sowars* rode up amongst the carts, cutting down unarmed men, till they were met by the guard, which succeeded in repelling them, but not without the loss of an officer and several men.

A section of the 78th poured in a death dealing volley, which strewed the road with men and horses; our horse battery and volunteer troop also swept the plain; but the enemy had made good his retreat.

Night fell, and was as usual accompanied by a rolling musketry-fire along our line of piquet's, while our bivouac, which had been already thrown back beyond the range of the hostile guns, was occasionally visited by a round shot, that rolled amongst the small tents, of which a limited supply had been furnished to the troops. Not without many an anxious feeling for the morrow, we betook ourselves to rest, thankful for having partaken once again of a hearty meal.

Our baggage-stores, after the attack which I have attempted to describe, were moved into the Alum Bagh, where they were secure from molestation.

The commissariat also lodged there, and the troops not on duty made it their resting-place during the night. The hospital also was opened in the Alum Bagh.

CHAPTER 11

The Battle to Relieve Lucknow

September 25th

The Alum Bagh, an enclosure of considerable extent, comprises a large mansion built of brick, with a mosque and Immaum barrack, contiguous, together with some insignificant out-houses. A well, of limpid purity and refreshing coolness, reposes beneath the broad shade of a magnificent building, rich in the numerous quaint devices of oriental taste. A garden, luxuriant in flower and shrub, and also a fine demesne, extending to the main road, encircle the entire, which one regretted should become the scene of strife. Having dislodged the enemy from hence on the previous day, we now occupied it ourselves. Our possession, however, was not long undisturbed, for no sooner had the morning dawned, than the Alum Bagh was made the object of fire from a battery visible to us from the roof only, but completely concealed on the plain by an overgrowth of com, which afforded it the cover of its rank luxuriance. The enemy, notwithstanding, failed in doing us any serious injury.

To hold the Alum Bagh, it was determined that two hundred and fifty men should be placed under the command of Lieutenant Colonel McIntyre, of the 78th. This, together with our losses on the 23rd, amounting to upwards of sixty officers and six men killed and wounded, greatly reduced our column of attack, which was formed at eight a.m., ready to advance on Lucknow. Never can I forget the appearance of that little band on this eventful occasion. Toil, privation, and exposure had left traces on the forms of our men, and yet daring, hope and energy seemed depicted on their countenances.

As I surveyed their ranks, I felt convinced that we should be able, ere night, to reach the Residency of Lucknow. I imparted this conviction to a brother officer, with whom I was talking during the conference of the Generals, which seemed of unusual length, so impatient were we for action. At length was spoken that word, so welcome to every heart in our united and determined band, "forward!"

The first brigade, General Neil's, with heavy guns, took the lead. It was composed of Her Majesty's 5th Fusiliers, Madras Fusiliers, 84th, a detachment of the 64th, and Olphert's Horse Battery. It followed the road leading to the city by the Char Bagh Bridge.

We had only advanced a short distance, when guns, commanding the road, opened from front and flanks, which, together with a musket fire from a large enclosed building filled by the enemy, made each advancing step one of great peril. While the head of our column checked this opposition, the succeeding regiments were ordered to lie down, the road above the level of the plain being greatly exposed.

It was fringed on either side by a row of young trees. I found cover behind one of these, about nine inches in girth, occasionally taking a shot as the mutineers appeared at doors or windows to give their fire.

In this situation our men were so much exposed, and our casualties were so numerous, that it was a relief afterwards to advance. Onwards they rushed, like an impetuous torrent, bearing down every obstacle, and braving every danger; nor did they slacken their speed till they reached the enemy's guns, which they captured at the point of the bayonet, killing his gunners or putting them to flight. The enemy was also obliged, by the valiant 5th Fusiliers, to abandon the house from whence, behind doors and windows, he had lately kept up a destructive fire, and thus the bridge was won.

Our adversaries seemed paralysed—there was a pause in the

firing—it ceased altogether. Still, though flushed by success, we were not insensible to danger, for we had to advance through a street of some length, on each side of which stood rows of houses. There was something suspicious—nay, sinister—in their aspect. We had, however, no time for dwelling upon such fancies. Our object was not yet attained, but must be won from death, which seemed to lower on the 'devoted garrison, and also on ourselves. What of that? We are not to be baffled—it shall be relieved! My pulse throbbed with wild excitement.

On into the street we rushed. A perfect storm of musketry, thick as hail, burst forth from doors, windows, and from flat roofs above our heads. Every aperture belched out fire; still onward rushed our hardy men, undaunted. No hesitation or confusion was there amongst them. Cool and composed, they preserved their sections of forces, mindful only of what was to be effected, and resolute on its performance.

The rear brigade, with Generals Outram and Havelock, having joined us, a pause ensued, of which the enemy took advantage to collect, and hang upon our rear.

On observing this, two regiments were immediately detached for the purpose of resisting any demonstration on his part, as well as for the protection of our heavy guns, now an immense encumbrance, hampering our progress, when to push on with the utmost celerity consistent with the preservation of good order and safety was imperative.

This delay, after the successful manner in which we had forced the main street, seemed to act on the enemy as a stimulant to renew the attack, for he opened a withering fire upon the head of our column from his various lurking-places; nor did it encourage our confidence. At last, making a counter-march, we quitted the street, led by Sir James Outram, and pursued a rough, uneven way, which skirted the deep ravine, already crossed by us, over the Char Bagh Bridge, and which opened into an avenue near the king's stables and *bazaar*. The ground on our left flank was steep and abrupt, thickly studded with sugar-cane, but fortunately unoccupied by the enemy.

For some time the only obstacle we encountered was the ruggedness of the way, and the consequent difficulty of bringing along our heavy guns, their progress being frequently interrupted by ruts, from which they required to be extricated, a work performed with much activity and goodwill by the Sikh Regiment of Ferozepore.

On this particular day, a fine spirit was manifested by that regiment, caused, perhaps, by the prospect of plunder, to which the Sikhs are extremely addicted. The sturdy 78th Highlanders, meantime, were busily engaged with the enemy, who closed upon the route we had taken. A part of our adversaries now made their appearance on the opposite side of the ravine, but were so overawed by the Sikh Regiment, that they remained concealed in the thick sugar-cane, while we steadily pushed onwards through narrow and intricate lanes and byways, which we found deserted and quite undefended. These led to the *bazaar*, where we came upon another portion of them; but we speedily forced them out of it Here we again halted, to close up the column.

Having found some hay under the veranda of a *serai*, we gladly appropriated it to our use, and reposed upon it with a keener sense of enjoyment than that of the Sybarite luxuriating on couch of down. How grateful that rest was, it would be impossible to imagine, except under similar circumstances.

In this advance Sir James Outram, ever conspicuous where fighting was hottest, was slightly wounded. So little did he make of the injury which he had received, that there was some difficulty in prevailing upon him to have it attended to. The colours of one regiment after another of the Oude Irregulars were brought in and presented to him. These had been taken in front, by the 5th Fusiliers and their brave brother soldiers of the Madras Regiment.

Many loose horses were also secured and brought into camp. I was presented with one of them by a piper of the 78th, a humorous fellow, who, in giving it to me, observed, that he thought I wanted a charger.

Captain Johnson, 5th Fusiliers, who had greatly distinguished himself during our progress, unfortunately was severely wounded while leading his company, as his men said, wherever the firing was hottest.

A large massive gate near the king's stables delayed our further advance by the barrier it offered, and such was its strength, that for a time it resisted the efforts of Captain Olpherts, who was foremost with the men of his battery to blow it open. At length it yielded to his endeavours, and the insurgents, who had been concealed within it, were dispatched. This act being notified to Sir James Outram, the column pushed on, regaining what appeared the principal road to the palaces; but we were again exposed to a deadly fire, which checked our advance, whilst our heavy guns sternly replied.

Here the cannonade was in the highest degree animating, and the excitement absorbing and supreme, while every building, loop-holed, swarmed with armed men, and literally bristled with muskets and matchlocks. On all sides we were exposed to their incessant fire; the missiles of death rained thick and fast among us. Shelter was unattainable, destruction imminent. Still we bore onward, but without the certainty of that brave garrison, for whose existence we had dared so much, being yet alive; for amidst all our dangers, hope grew strong and cheered us.

Nerving our hearts against the tide of opposition, we advanced steadily till we reached a large courtyard.

And now it was proved that notwithstanding the surprise of the insurgents at the unexpected route we had pursued, they were nevertheless prepared for us. Their artillery bore upon us along the line of road by the river Goomtee, till we at length diverged through a plantation, and resumed the road to the Residency, by crossing a low bridge. We descended to it, and came out again at the centre; the *nullagh*, which it spanned, being dry, and the parapet so low as to enable us to step over.

This, indeed, was not the least dangerous part of the advance, as it was commanded by the mess-house, from which a withering fire of musketry was poured upon us. To escape this we dispersed, and, *chacun pour soi*, rushed singly over the bridge to get within the cover of a high wall of one of the palaces.

Those who had first crossed had taken possession of a house, from an angle of which they kept up a brisk fire, to cover the remainder. As my turn came to cross the bridge, it seemed quite a chance to me that I should ever reach the other side; for we had all to scramble up from the *nullagh*, and I had almost doubted the capabilities of my horse, as he rose to jump over the parapet. One false step, and both were lost. Besides this, the dark colour of my uniform offered so strong a contrast to the light tints of the prevailing colouring, that it afforded a fair target to the marksmen, one scarce possible to miss in such a heavy fire. Still an Almighty Providence led me on unscathed.

The rear was now brought up by our heavy battery, though I feared at one time that our line of communication had been lost by our wounded and rear-guard, as we saw neither during the time we halted near some deserted buildings. When they reached us, there was much confusion, so that horse, foot, guns, camels, bullocks, *palanquins*, and *dhoolies*, for the sick and wounded, were all united in an inextricable mass of disorder.

The opportunity to rest, though at first acceptable to the wearied soldiers, soon became irksome, so great was their eagerness to reach our desired goal, the Baillie Guard.

This was evident from the numerous murmurs amongst the mass of men now exposed to the enemy's fire in several directions. We seemed to be at fault for want of a guide, when the brave young Havelock, nephew to our general, valiant as his sire, who poured out his life on the sanguinary field of Chillianwallah, unable to resist the excitement of the moment, suddenly exclaimed: "For God's sake, let us go on, sir."

The troops were re-formed, and, venting their feelings in one unanimous and hearty cheer, dashed impetuously through the archway which leads into the Khas *bazaar*, though assailed by a storm of musketry, kept up without intermission, as each regiment pushed on. In this advance my horse was wounded, his hind leg being pierced by a bullet, while another rattled down upon one of my holsters. I grieve to record that Lieutenant Joley, 32nd Regiment, was mortally wounded in this advance. I was fortunate in being able to expedite the progress of my friend Captain Johnson's (5th Fusiliers) *dhoolie* bearers, being otherwise unoccupied; and, while thus engaged, I conversed with the brave and determined General Neil for the last time, who observed to me as he sat his horse, near the archway: "I shall see the rear of my brigade forward, it is getting dark." I never saw him alive again.

Further delay took place in finding out the entrance to the Residency, and then in removing a portion of the barricades which impeded our advance.

While this was being effected, we again rested, the moon rising calm and bright above us, and looking down coldly on our entry, when, at length, all obstacles were removed.

The time we had been engaged in this undertaking was eleven hours, during which our troops had been without refreshment, and were exposed to manifold dangers, seen and unseen. All this they bore without a murmur, for they were bent on the attainment of an object which they nobly accomplished; and then they looked upon it as an all-sufficient reward to have relieved those brave men who had hitherto struggled against such fearful odds, and had maintained a position rendered tenable only by their individual valour and surpassing energy.

The mess-room of the dauntless 32nd was hospitably opened to us, and their last drop of wine given to us. The hardships of the siege were but too plainly written on the wan, attenuated features of the garrison, both men and women—the latter a noble example of the fortitude and endurance of which, in times of trial, the sex is capable, and a proof of their being well worthy of the defence made for them by husbands and friends.

Nor was this memorable struggle confined alone to the military. Every civilian did duty under arms; and, very probably, the spirit which animated the whole of the besieged may have gone far to make up for the paucity of their numbers.

Quick in succession were the reports of round-shot fired on

the building where we sat with our new friends, the enemy's attack on the entrenchments being unabated. But our advance had been most timely—it saved the garrison. The Residency had been completely undermined, and the delay of even a day would have proved fatal.

September 26th

With morning came the recollection that our wounded, together with the heavy guns, were in the rear, upon which the insurgent *sowars* had closed.

Many instances of bravery were shown by the escort in defence of these poor, helpless men. Well did staunch soldiers, on this occasion, merit the Victoria Cross for which they were recommended, so valiantly did they strive to resist hundreds by whom they were beset.

Most unhappily, about some twenty of the wounded, in rear of the others, were basely deserted by the cowardly *dhoolie*-bearers (natives), who fled, leaving their helpless charge to the tender mercies of the demoniacal Sepoys, whose atrocities they were utterly unable to resist, and by whom—horrible to relate—they were burnt to death.

An appalling lesson this on the urgent necessity for careful avoidance of all straggling on the line of march! This straggling should be strictly prohibited, especially during hostilities; and a strict communication should be preserved with the front. To the neglect of this precaution, too many valuable lives were sacrificed.

The bringing-in of the wounded, as well as the heavy guns, which ought to have followed the night before, cost much bloodshed. Colonel Campbell, C.B., in command of the 90th—a most distinguished officer—was, upon this occasion, severely wounded, and, I lament to add, died, after suffering amputation of the leg. For promptitude and vigour of action, cool judgment, and impetuous bravery, he was pre-eminent.

Such a man could ill be spared from the service at any time, particularly now, when qualities such as those by which he was characterised are so much needed. Major Cooper also fell. We lost Captain Pakenham, 84th, on the preceding day. He was a most able officer and devoted soldier; he was killed in entering the city, after storming the bridge. Of him it might, with truth, be said, that he "foremost fighting fell."

On the 29th September, and following days, some spirited sorties took place, by which we gained a more advantageous position along the river, including the Taree Kothe, Furradh Bucsh, and Chuttur Munzil palaces. These were immediately occupied by the gallant 78th, 84th, 64th, and Sikh Regiment, under two brigadiers, the entire being under the command of General Havelock.

The original garrison of Lucknow, under Brigadier Inglis, was strengthened by a portion of the bold Madras Fusiliers. Not a man was to be spared, each separate post being held by the smallest number possible; and how they succeeded in maintaining them is a matter of astonishment, considering the fearful odds to which they were opposed.

Our wounded amounted to five hundred and fifty in number, exclusive of sixty officers, since our little force left Cawnpore. It was a most painful reflection that for these brave men, who deserved so much in return for the unsparing manner in which they had exposed their lives, no secure resting-place could be obtained, the whole of the Residency being in a tottering condition. Every place was perforated with shot and shell, and perpetually exposed to the influence of the enemy's batteries, so that, after admission into the several large buildings used as hospitals, many of the occupants were either killed or wounded. Every adjacent space of ground, swarming with camp-followers and cattle, was subject to the effects of the numerous mortar-batteries, by which man and beast were frequently destroyed. Many of the wounded suffered piteously, despite the persevering and anxious efforts of Dr. Scott, 32nd, superintending, to better their condition. Still there was no remedy, the number of beds was insufficient, and days elapsed before those required could be supplied. The fortitude of the wounded was almost sublime, while our hearts ached for the sufferings, which it was beyond our power to mitigate.

We were now placed upon reduced rations, limited to two scanty meals a day, barely sufficient to support existence, without allaying hunger; nor had we any stimulant whatsoever, with the exception of tea, which was attainable only to a few. The lowering effect of this diet was speedily apparent, as it was inadequate to supply the waste occasioned by overwrought physical exertion. It developed illness of a painful and debilitating character, against which it was almost impossible to struggle, and from which, in common with many others, I suffered myself.

Meantime, the adverse batteries continued to play upon us with little intermission. Throughout the night we were disturbed by the fire of small arms, together with shouting and the shrill discordant sound of native music at intervals, all close to our entrenchments. Such disturbance effectually banished sleep, and kept us quite on the *qui vive* lest the apparently impending attack should be made and find us unprepared. Nor was this the only mode of torment devised for us by the fiendish temper of our foe, ingenious in petty malice.

Knowing how straitened we were for food on several occasions, they hoisted cakes on the ends of long poles, high above the walls which separated us from them—taunting us with our destitution, and predicting how many days we had yet to live. We have also been annoyed with swarms of flies.

The place is literally alive with all sorts and sizes of flies, some of them sleek and others bloated, apparently gorged with putridity, and thriving in this pestilential atmosphere, which swelters with mortality.

They taint and pollute everything. Even our scant allowance of sorry food is rendered yet more abhorrent to us from their vile contact, till even the appetite which craves food rejects such food with disgust.

Nor does the evil stop here, for they increase the sufferings of the sick and the torture of the wounded.

My poor friend, the brave Captain Johnson, 5th Fusiliers, is no more. He possessed all the elements that constitute a true soldier. Sincerely did I mourn as I followed him to his early grave; though it is a melancholy consolation to me to reflect that I spared him a night's exposure to the cruel foe, and had the privilege of seeking to mitigate his sufferings. I knew him from his boyhood. He held his first commission in the 60th, where he was the object of much regard. On many occasions he performed far more than what mere duty required, till at length, in the prime and flower of manhood, he died as became a soldier. He was, however, not only esteemed for his soldier-like qualities, but he was also beloved by all who knew his genial nature.

CHAPTER 12

The Besieged Garrison

OCTOBER 1ST

We are still exposed to the enemy's batteries. In a sortie made towards the Cawnpore battery we suffered loss. Our outposts are held by three regiments and two brigadiers, the palace being in possession of the rebels.

The foresight and prudence of Sir Henry Lawrence showed themselves in laying up a large store of provisions here, which have been most useful to us, cut off as we are at present from the possibility of obtaining supplies. No communication between this and the Alum Bagh is practicable, nor are we free from apprehension of an attack on that post being made by the enemy.

It is now decided that five thousand fresh troops must arrive to complete what only half that number undertook, destitute alike of cavalry and horse artillery.

Our ammunition is scarce, which acts as a great restraint upon the use of our artillery. We can make no impression without shelling the town, which is enormous in extent, and massively built. We can hold no line of communication with our rear and baggage, while spies make great difficulty in undertaking our messages, even when heavily paid for bringing us tidings from without.

OCTOBER 2ND

The adverse batteries still continue to play upon us, and seldom can we reply from our entrenchments.

At midnight, a fire of musketry, matchlocks, and gingals, kept us for some time under arms, but, contrary to our expectation, no assault was made. Yesterday I found myself elected prize agent, much to my surprise, and without even knowing that my name had been proposed to the prize committee, which it was found necessary to form for the proper disposal of the vast amount of treasure discovered in the royal palaces. This treasure consists of moneys, precious stones, and a variety of the most heterogeneous description of property, comprising ivory, silver, copper, and other metals, linen and cooking utensils.

But before the necessary measures were taken for securing these effects, the most valuable had been abstracted. Sergeant Staunton, Her Majesty's 84th Regiment, has shown great assiduity and vigilance in assisting to collect and store the property.

The quantity of linen discovered is ample, and will materially add to the comforts of the sick and wounded. The number of requisitions that we have already attended to, is surprising.

October 3rd

Three guns and a battery have been destroyed by us, which, with the effect of a mine, caused the enemy some loss. The garrison continues to supply our entire force with provisions, there being no possibility of obtaining what we require otherwise, and any attempt at forage deemed impracticable.

Sunday, October 4th

Divine service was performed at noon, and again at three, p.m. The attack from the hostile batteries continues unabated.

October 5th

At midnight our cavalry were ordered to make an attempt to reach Alum Bagh, under Captain Barrow.

This, however, was frustrated by the enemy, who had assembled a strong force on the bank of the river, from whence he immediately opened fire on observing our party, which fortunately retired without loss.

On the succeeding day the enemy obliged our advanced picquet, to which he had pushed up, to withdraw; he also threw up batteries on the opposite bank of the river, and he now maintains the strictest surveillance. We have, however, been cheered by the report that a brigade from Allahabad is advancing into Oude.

Hemmed in as the garrison has been, it is little wonder that this news should be most welcome. An escape from the tainted, foetid atmosphere we now breathe would indeed be a relief, for nothing can be more loathsome. Its horrible impurities are sickening, and it is a wonder that some dire pestilence is not engendered by the quantity of decomposing animal matter which infects the air. To enforce anything like proper sanitary measures seems utterly hopeless.

The Dewaler festival is approaching, and has been announced by the rebels as the most propitious time for attacking us successfully. The existence of this intention was also announced to us by our chiefs.

On the night of the 18th, and the preceding one, there was a great deal of firing but the enemy made no advance.

October 19th.

Maun Sing, the insurgent commander has made proposals with the view of securing his life and property, while he maintains his followers in the city, and prepares batteries on the opposite bank, bearing directly upon the entrenchments. One stands on a small mound stockaded in the centre and covered by the strong wall of the enclosure.

Grain can no longer be supplied by the commissariat for our horses or cattle, and it is piteous to see how lean the poor things have become.

The advanced of more troops from Cawnpore is deferred by the commander-in-chief till the arrival of regiments from Calcutta, and a month of blockade and privation seems inevitable.

It is melancholy that the women and children should be exposed to this, though nothing can be more admirable than the fortitude displayed by the former. Each individual seems a heroine.

The worst suffering must be that endured by parents seeing their children pining, wasting, dying, without the power of procuring the necessary remedy, fresh sweet air, or wholesome nutritious food.

Poor wee things! They seem quite to have reconciled themselves to their doleful situation, and even form mimic batteries for their amusement, and talk, during their play, of shot and shell.

We had hoped for relief earlier, a small number of fugitives from Delhi had been ordered to join us here, but have been detained at Cawnpore in search of insurgents in that district.

Soon after the p.m. a sudden and intense discharge of musketry shot and shell occurred but soon ceased; nor was it an experience like that of Sunday again, which lasted for three-quarters of an hour.

Bugle calls are generally sounded for withdrawal, a signal which our practiced ear has now taught us to recognise.

Intelligence has reached us of the approach of troops from Allahabad, so that in a week our blockade may be removed by their dispatch.

The enemy entrench themselves within three hundred yards of our outposts, and in a parallel direction.

We learn from the report of spies that they are dejected and bereft of confidence; yet, while we cannot make any attempt to dislodge them on our side, they have contrived, by mining, to destroy two of our sentries posted in a house. It is alleged that their intention had been discovered and reported by the party who were holding the post, but, most unfortunately, not thereupon withdrawn.

Since storming the city, the strength of the corps is again greatly reduced by losses in killed and wounded by attacks on subsequent days. Our force is now too weak to act otherwise than on the defensive, as additional casualties would overwork those left for duty. So many officers have either fallen or been wounded, that a proportion equal to duty is not available; and an assault upon the Residency, in force, could only be met by a few men of different regiments mixed up together.

The variation of temperature here is particularly trying to the health of the troops. At night they are exposed to great and oppressive heat, which at dawn changes to extreme cold. They have neither bedding nor great-coats, spirits nor tobacco. Yet they endure these privations with a degree of sturdy cheerfulness the most admirable. The intensity of the sun at midday is absolutely torturing.

So far we have lived through a time of great excitement.

One of our English humorists has said, "suspense is a miserable thing, it is the life of a spider;" and spider-like, in truth, has our existence been since we entered this place.

Our life has been dependent upon as frail a tenure as the commiserated spider's, shot and shell flying about us, without any lengthened intermission, for the past two days; during the forenoon killing an apothecary and mortally wounding one of the patients in the hospital. Mines too have been sprung by the enemy, and a man has been blown up. Our defences have not been improved, and a scarcity of ammunition causes us to refrain from mounting more guns.

Our security seems to lie in the timidity of the insurgents, whose numerical superiority does not inspire them with courage to attack the position; an assault upon which in such force would be the destruction of our weak garrison. The resources of the enemy in artillery, and especially in shells, place us in a very helpless position, without the prospect of succour.

OCTOBER 23RD

A post near the iron bridge leading to the rebel camp, and only two hundred and fifty yards from it, has been taken.

The enemy has at length menaced our rear-guard and baggage, and carried off some of our elephants; nor is this our sole misfortune.

Intelligence has been received from Cawnpore that the line of our expected reinforcements has been either interrupted, or their approach rendered difficult by an insurgent force being in possession of the road from thence to Lucknow. The enemy has removed his batteries to a greater distance, and has thereby obtained a more correct range, which makes his fire of greater effect; while so sparing are we compelled by necessity to be of our ammunition, that we are forced to use it in reduced charges.

OCTOBER 26TH

It is just one month since the troops under Generals Outram and Havelock forced their way into Lucknow. The former has the military command of two divisions—Dinapore and Cawnpore, as well as Rajpootana—and is also chief commissioner of Oude.

No other general officer is at hand, and all movements await the instruction of the commander-in-chief. Meanwhile, a number of mutineers, advancing upon Cawnpore from Gwalior, is stated, by messengers, to have sustained a complete defeat before our troops from that station.

Yesterday, our scale of daily rations was reduced, in order to make them suffice for a month.

Several countermines are being made by our laborious engineers to counteract those of the enemy.

I have been struck on the left foot by a musket ball, while sitting on the bed of a friend, with whom I was conversing. This has somewhat crippled me for the present; but among so many who are badly wounded, I have great reason for thankfulness not to have suffered more.

Yesterday evening, the last of my candles burnt out! My entire store consisted of three, which I husbanded most carefully. I never properly estimated the value of artificial light before, and can now most feelingly enter into the preference expressed for it by that quaint humorist, the gentle Elia. How often have I smiled at his strange conceits!

Hail! candle-light—mild viceroy of the moon!

Tonight, I shall utter this in vain, for there will be no "mild viceroy of the moon" to cheer me with its light. I should not mind this so much, if able to move about. However, considering that I rarely kept my candles lighted longer than from five to ten minutes, I have not very much reason for grumbling.

The insurgents continue to salute us every morning, soon after dawn, with a few rounds from their batteries. They use wooden shells, which seem harmless.

Ever since the 7th, I have been emulating "the little busy bee," whose industrious habits have been immortalised by Watts for the benefit of small urchins in the nursery; but, instead of "gathering honey all the day," which, in the innocence of my childhood, I considered rather a sensual enjoyment on the part of this same lauded little insect, I have been improving and shining here in giving instructions in the manufacture of Enfield rifle cartridges, and superintending the same. It seemed such a pity to have so valuable and efficient a weapon as the Enfield rifle in abeyance for lack of ammunition—the more especially as our men had used it with so much success during our advance, that they were reluctant to dally with the somewhat antiquated Brown Bess, after having been so faithfully served by her Enfield rival—that I volunteered to undertake the service of superintending the manufacture of Enfield rifle cartridges.

I established a factory at the Baillie Guard, near my prize store, flung pink tape to the winds, and have been busily engaged for eight hours every day, assisted by Lieutenant Sewell, who fortunately possessed a bullet-mould, which he lent me, and whom I found a most apt pupil. He receives an allowance of twenty-five pounds per month in compensation, which is as little as can be offered, considering the utility of the service and the risk which it involves. So exposed is this place, and so highly inflammable are the ingredients in use, that we are liable at any moment to be blown up; but the knowledge of our danger teaches our men caution.

One poor fellow, I grieve to say, was shot dead today at this work in the veranda, and a Highlander also wounded by the same shot. My foot aches a great deal; the muscle has been hit. I am crippled by it, but am not, I am thankful to add, incapacitated from performing my twofold duty of prize agent and cartridge maker.

I resigned my appointment as deputy judge advocate to the

force, lest it might interfere to prevent me from bestowing the necessary attention upon the manufacture of this ammunition, even though told that I might still retain the office. However, I do not like monopoly in any form, or under any circumstances, and could not therefore consistently practice it, which proof of my sincerity costs me forty pounds per month.

A convoy with further supply of provisions has reached Alum Bagh! The troops there must absolutely revel in abundance, while we are acquiring something very like correct practical knowledge of starvation, as certain gastronomic reminiscences, fraught with the savoury odours of the "fleshpots of Egypt," rise in mockery of our scanty portion of tough gun-bullock, sacrificed to appease the cravings of our hunger, and escape the gnawing of its own.

Most truly can each individually exclaim with the psalmist— *My bones look out and stare upon me.*

We have become as gaunt and lean as possible; but the wretched horses and cattle are even in worse plight. I never see the poor creatures without commiseration. Thanks to a kindly rajah, I have become the possessor of two *siers* of sugar—a splendid acquisition in these times. It now sells for sixteen *rupees* per *sier*, I have bought as good for sixpence.

October 27th

Poor Groydon, of the Bengal Army, has been mortally wounded at his post. Most nobly had he, at all times and on all occasions, performed his duty; he was an officer whose loss can be ill supplied. How many valuable lives this dire mutiny has cost us!

The insurgent chief, the Rajah Maun Singh, is again trying to make terms with us; but we pay no attention to his overtures. Intelligence from Cawnpore reports the approach of the Delhi column under Colonel Greathed, and the defeat of a rebel force at Soorajpore by the troops holding Cawnpore, but without being able to prevent the insurgents carrying off their guns.

It is stated that six English, including two ladies and as many children, have been brought as prisoners into the city this day. Our rations here are now reduced to eight ounces of meat daily, with two ounces of *ghee* every alternate day. Our casualties are numerous. Dr. Darby has been badly wounded by a piece of shell.

OCTOBER 28TH

The fire from the batteries and mortars is still kept up, the shells being made of stone or wood, the former well formed.

The insurgents announce their intention of making a final assault upon our position, which they predict will be fatal to us. It is also reported that the followers of the Rajah Maun Singh are, at his instance, withdrawing from the attack. We have received the government despatch relative to the taking of Delhi suburbs. It returns the loss on our side as amounting to eleven hundred, which is light in comparison with that of the force under General Havelock in advancing upon Lucknow with numbers much inferior.

Our rear-guard has been again supplied with a fresh store of provisions from Cawnpore, at which place troops are assembling, both from Delhi and Calcutta, for the second relief of Lucknow; while an insurgent force is reported to be advancing upon Cawnpore to divert the relieving army from approaching this place.

The fire from outside has become more regular and sustained; there are shells and round shot, for about two hours, morning and evening, with a protracted fire of musketry at night.

OCTOBER 30TH

I received intimation from the Alum Bagh, that an English letter to my address was there. Observing my solicitude to obtain it, my servant, Mahomet Ali, (I record the kindness with pleasure) immediately volunteered to go out for it, though the service is one of danger. If he succeeds in his object, he will have shown no small address.

Few have been able to go out from hence, so closely are we

invested, and so extraordinary is the vigilance of our foes, especially at night. Nothing can exceed the virulence of the old Sepoys against us, and, compared with them, the armed people of Oude are mild "as sucking doves." The lax state of discipline observed in the native army, coupled with the annexation of Oude, has mainly led to rebellion. A native army should be allowed to number only one-third of our forces; and the strictest discipline should be maintained by officers, whose sole interest should be in their several regiments. Indifference and apathy in this particular have mainly contributed to the extensive disaffection which prevails.

In reorganising the native army, the existence of which will be ever necessary for the maintenance of our Indian empire, the first step should be to provide both judicious and active commanding officers, who would look into the interior economy of their several regiments, impress their subordinates with a just sense of the responsibility attached to their relative positions, and inculcate the conscientious discharge of their several duties. The performance of these duties with exactitude and punctuality would ensure the growth and preservation of discipline, and effectually prevent a recurrence of the disasters to which self-interest and a fatal system of *laissez aller* have conduced. A certain class of men repudiate the idea of professional earnestness; men such as these should never enter the service.

November 3rd

I am miserably anxious about my poor servant, Mahomet Ali. Should he have fallen a victim to his kind wish to relieve my anxiety by bringing me my English letter, I should deplore having consented to his making the attempt, which was very selfish of me, I must confess. The debility against which I struggle is extreme; I do not recollect to have experienced anything so prostrating before, and yet I exert my will to the very utmost.

The rebel batteries have been in play more than usual; their range has much improved. Two of our brave Highlanders were hit today from sheer exposure one was killed by a musket-bullet on the spot, while the man standing next to him was mortally wounded by an open breach in the wall. The many deaths resulting from incautiousness prove how familiarity with danger deadens the perception of its existence. In vain have our men been warned of the necessity of caution, to ensure their own safety.

Such a relief it was to me, when I awoke this morning, a little before dawn, to see coiled up on the floor, near the foot of my bed, my faithful Mahomet Ali, apparently exhausted by fatigue. On awaking, he told me he had found it impossible to proceed, despite repeated attempts to escape the vigilance of the enemy, and had most reluctantly returned, his mission unperformed.

Today, Lieutenant Dashwood, who had already been wounded, was struck by a round shot in both legs, as he was sketching outside the entrenchments, under the guns of the enemy, by whom he must have been observed from the opposite bank. There seems but feeble prospect of his recovery.

On the second of this month we succeeded in destroying a stockade by one of our batteries; such an advantage rarely occurs, as our guns are generally silent.

Intelligence of Sir Colin Campbell's arrival at Cawnpore has reached us, as well as the advance of the force in relief. Plans also have been communicated of the mode to be adopted in their advance, so as to frustrate the designs of the insurgents, and nullify the obstacles caused by them to render the direct road impracticable. The difficulties of this route we know but too well, having already penetrated it, and learnt thereby that an advancing column, without flanking parties, makes small impression on troops fighting behind stone walls, and is also quite unable to make them abandon the upper stories of the houses, from whence they can deliver their fire effectively, while our men are firing at them through windows with difficulty. The space occupied by this city is about fifteen miles in circumference.

According to my opinion, the *bazaars* held by the insurgents should be invested, till the town was rendered untenable by shelling, while our troops should, by a flank march, carry the cantonment batteries by attack from rear, and the approaches to both bridges towards the north and east, and should then enter and maintain possession of the city in such bodies as the extent and amount of opposition shown might demand.

Cavalry and artillery, ready for swift pursuit, should hold the different lines of retreat, with a force at south and west, to co-operate and intercept fugitives, to whom, if Sepoys and armed men, no quarter should be given. This severity would be a lesson on the cruelties generally executed on their own officers and helpless families, in sparing neither age nor sex, and in being deaf to all entreaty.

The city thus invested, the enemy would be compelled to make a sortie, perhaps in more directions than one, and meet our troops on the plain. Once in collision with them, the issue would not long be doubtful.

November 7th

This is the forty-third day of our investment by the rebels.

For three days, their batteries have played at intervals upon our position.

Last night we received positive information of the advance of Sir Colin Campbell, with the force from Delhi, and also fresh troops from England, said altogether to amount to six thousand infantry, six hundred cavalry, and thirty-six guns, to join our rear-guard and baggage at the Alum Bagh. It was expected that they would reach that place on the 10th instant.

Be it observed that seven months had elapsed since the outbreak of the Indian mutiny, before the first portion of troops from England could take the field.

How shall the services of those brave few, who bore the burden and heat of the day, be recognised in England?

The staff now here consists of a garrison and brigade staff (the original Lucknow staff), the staff of the Oude field force, and the staff of the several divisions. So loosely were matters conducted, that the first-mentioned did not even keep a garrison-roster till lately. Nor were charges for courts-martial framed by the adjutant-general's department, in the absence of any judge advocate.

Any number of authorities, including a medical officer, were permitted to supervise proceedings, and remit or hasten the punishment awarded by drum-head courts-martial, so called. Upon one occasion, in the framing of a charge, as I am credibly informed, *jam*, with other *edibles*, was called articles of *bedding*.

The amount of plunder taken here, before the arrival of our relieving force, must have been enormous. An immense quantity of property belonging to the king, together with costly pearls, was deposited in the entrenchment occupied when the bold step of holding out with insufficient guns was determined upon by Sir Henry Lawrence. Subsequently to the abandonment of the fortified camp at Muchee Bawan, these treasures were shamefully pillaged. A portion, however, of the crown jewels escaped from this general plunder, and have been secured.

Much of this loss has been attributed to the number of Europeans and uncovenanted people, who at the time sought protection within the entrenchments, and who, with their natural avidity, profited by the occasion, which was perhaps too tempting to be resisted. They quickly possessed themselves of many coveted valuables, and have continued to hold large quantities of property with the greatest impunity.

Her Majesty's regiments, also, which furnished the guard and sentries for the protection of the jewels and treasure, and for the conveyance of them into the entrenchments, possessed themselves of a considerable portion. They were even known individually to have offered them for sale, and had not yet been compelled to deliver them over, though admonished to do so, by a special general order.

On the arrival of the relieving force conducted by Generals Sir James Outram and Havelock the public quarters given over or occupied by regiments were stripped of stores of valuable property. In many instances, this property was wantonly destroyed. Even the places where, by aid of masonry, gold, silver, and jewels had been deposited, were broken into and plundered by the soldiers.

When a prize committee was hastily selected, it was discovered that a large amount of treasure had been lost. The defence urged is, that no order in prohibition of such licence was issued—but it would be difficult to excuse the conduct of men, who, when the enemy was near at hand, quitted their ranks or posts in search of plunder.

On Sunday we had divine service at twelve o'clock, and again at three, p.m., during which the rebel batteries were silent, but opened again in the evening.

Throughout the succeeding night, the fire of small arms was incessant. In the morning, the rebels commenced firing briskly from their batteries, killing and wounding some of our men in the entrenchment. A poor Sepoy, one of the faithful few, was mortally wounded whilst on sentry. Next day, the forty-seventh of our investment, Mr. Cavanagh, a volunteer, boldly ventured to assume a native disguise, and, eluding the vigilance of the foe, reached the Alum Bagh, where a flag was hoisted to notify to us his safe arrival. He brought useful information to the commander-in-chief, and also offered his services as guide. We were now all elated at the prospect of our speedy deliverance.

During the forenoon of the ensuing day, there was a good deal of heavy firing, which we thought might be occasioned by the van, under the commander-in-chief, engaging the insurgents. We found our conjecture right, for at two o'clock p.m., we learnt by telegraph, that two guns had been captured from the enemy, whose batteries had opened upon the Residency soon after five o'clock a.m. During the day, bodies of mutineers left the town by the stone bridge, with colours flying. These were, however, replaced by the entrance of about fifteen hundred infantry and some hundred cavalry.

It will be quite a matter of rejoicing for our native followers to leave this place. Poor creatures! They have been dreadfully hard pressed for lack of food, the quantity lately issued being

exceedingly limited, even considering their natural abstemious-
ness. Their endurance is greatly to be commended; they have
performed all work required of them, without grumbling.

As to my own attendant, Mahomed Ali, he is beyond praise,
doing everything for me with the hearty readiness of goodwill
and acting as water-carrier, *hamal* and baker, for he has volunteered to make bread for me. He has not only done all that I
required, but more; he has taken it upon himself to manufacture
the quaintest cap imaginable for my personal adornment, which
is quite a specimen of his ingenuity, and by wearing which I
have gratified him excessively.

On the fifty-second day of our investment, Monday the 16th,
after some cannonading between the advancing force and the
insurgents, during the afternoon, the signal was made of the
intention of his excellency, the commander-in-chief, to advance
next day.

Early in the forenoon, the sound of heavy and prolonged
fighting had tantalized us greatly, as it was a matter of difficulty
to espy the cause of it from our entrenchment. At eleven p.m.
and three a.m., the enemy mustered and kept up a discharge of
small arms on the entrenchment, without, however, making any
attempt at an attack; our mortars returned a few rounds in reply.
On the 9th, our sick and wounded had amounted to forty-two
officers and four hundred and fifty men, exclusive of one hundred non-combatants. One hundred is the total number of officers killed and wounded since the 12th of July, the date of our
first action with the enemy.

Wednesday, November 17th

Yesterday, our force advanced its position during the afternoon, acting in concert with the attack made by his excellency,
Sir Colin Campbell, and, under the cover of two batteries, obtained considerable advantage. Our loss in killed and wounded
numbered twenty. Lieutenant Ayton, Adjutant of the 84th, a
most gallant soldier, was severely wounded, and obliged to submit to amputation of the arm. At noon, operations on our side

were suspended, to facilitate the advance of the relieving force, with which a junction will be effected. This will enable us to get our bedding and clothes, of which we all stand greatly in need.

The batteries against the entrenchments keep up occasional mortar practice; but there will soon be an end of this; our release from this dreary imprisonment is at hand; and the blessing of sweet pure air will, after all we have endured while exposed to the present noxious atmosphere, be duly appreciated. Never was speedy change of quarters more needed. The old garrison and occupants of the entrenchments bear manifest tokens of what they have lived through, nor do the first relieving force appear less toil-worn; all wear the peculiar appearance of exposure to foul air and noisome exhalations.

The Baillie Guard, a small building, accommodates the garrison and fifty Sepoys, besides containing the treasury, prize store, and Enfield cartridge manufactory, while the few buildings in the position are occupied like a rabbit-warren. Every nook is full, and the open space, exposed as it is, day and night, to the enemy's fire, is thronged with cattle and native followers, though many of both have been killed since the investment commenced.

The greatest number of casualties took place just before the arrival of General Havelock's reinforcement, when the insurgents were within about sixty yards of the imperfect field-work, upon which their musketry almost daily played with deadly effect.

On the 21st November, the fifty-seventh day of our investment, at five o'clock p.m., I finally left the Baillie Guard. I was scarce able to crawl, so great were my debility and exhaustion, which bad and insufficient food, confinement, and foul air had produced. Still the delight which I experienced at the prospect of release from *durance vile*, lent me strength for the effort. I therefore quitted the Baillie Guard, under orders to proceed with prize property towards Cawnpore, and halt at Dilkoosha Park till the entire force should have assembled.

My route from the Residency lay through the different palaces and enclosures held by Havelock's troops since we arrived to save the garrison. This position had been further extended on one side to effect a junction with the commander-in-chief, and this part of the road was unavoidably exposed to the enemy's batteries from the opposite side of the Goomtee.

The advanced post of the Mathee Matial was occupied by the commander-in-chief's force. Here I found my old and esteemed brother officer, the Hon. Adrian Hope, who received me with a hospitable welcome, genial as his own fine nature. He made me partake of some bread and butter, a most welcome treat, as a long time had elapsed since I had had anything so dainty; also of some meat, cooked in a civilized fashion. After this refreshment I went on, still crossing the enemy's fire, till I found myself in the midst of a large bivouac, on either side of the road, with the river to one side.

Near the river were the headquarters of Sir Colin Campbell, the Secunder Bagh, memorable for the slaughter of seventeen hundred Sepoys the preceding day. They had been, much to their surprise, hemmed in by the 93rd Highlanders, part of the 53rd, and the Sikh regiment; by this force a terrible vengeance was executed in their destruction.

Immediately before I arrived, the enemy, in an attack made by him on one of our flanks, had been repulsed by a troop of our horse artillery and part of the 53rd, who set fire to his position. It was still in flames, in the midst of which one poor wretch, who, it was supposed, had been concealed by the thick bushes with which it was covered, was seen to spring up madly, as if to escape the devouring element, and was at once shot down.

I met several friends in the 53rd, who received me most kindly; we had last met in Calcutta. Since then a momentous time had elapsed. They all seemed flushed and elated by the opportunity now opened to them, and so ardently desired, of partaking in the campaign. Much did I envy them their position of being with their regiments.

At night the force was obliged to remain on the alert, for the place which it occupied was so exposed as to demand vigilance to guard against surprise.

Stretching myself upon my iron chair, I lay beside my charge in the little bivouac, under the shadow of a spreading tree near the Secunder Bagh. The spot which I had chosen for repose was alike unhealthy and insecure, for the air was tainted with the festering corpses of the slaughtered Sepoys, and our artillery had withdrawn from the range of the insurgents' batteries. Yet I was so overpowered by fatigue, weakness, and sickening effluvia that I was unable to exert myself to alter my position.

Morning light revealed to me the imminence of the danger which I had escaped, for the bole of the tree under which I lay was torn by shot.

During that night, 21st November, the wounded were withdrawn from the Residency, and escorted to the camp of the reserve, Dilkoosha Park. Though every precaution which kind consideration for their precarious state could suggest had been observed, this move proved fatal to many of their number. Amongst the losses thus incurred were the brave Major Stevenson, Madras Fusiliers, and the no less gallant Captain Boyle, 78th Highlanders.

The whole of the next day was employed in withdrawing the families. Many of the ladies received a kind welcome from the commander-in-chief, who gave them a resting-place at his headquarters, where they remained till, under cover of darkness, they were removed to Dilkoosha Park, whither I accompanied them, taking advantage of the escort. The distance which we traversed was about four miles. The route, which lay off the main road, was rough and uneven, very involved and intricate, and consequently rather difficult for the advance of a long train such as ours.

The escort consisted of the Irregular Horse and some Lancers, and seen in the dim night light, the entire cavalcade was wonderfully striking, novel, and picturesque; nor could there have been anything more full of excitement. We were obliged to halt frequently, because of the nature of the ground; and each time we stopped, those in the rear, unconscious of what was passing in front, suffered all the terrors of uncertainty. Yet we pursued our journey without the slightest molestation, and arrived safely at the camp of the 9th Lancers at the Dilkoosha Park, where we were heartily welcomed.

The families were regaled with a most profuse liberality. Food, such as they had been long without tasting, was set before them, and accordingly they did ample justice to it; indeed, so ravenous were they, that, according to the statement of the Khansommer of the 9th Lancers, on this one night, 23rd November, they consumed no less than twenty days' provision.

I was met on my arrival by my servants, after being two months separated from them, with kind expressions of satisfaction at my return. Each seemed eager to proffer his assistance, helping me to obtain the necessities of which I stood in need; wine, food, and also a cup of tea, were such an immense treat. In short, everything was ready for me that I would need. During the short time they had served me they seemed to have got a knowledge of my habits and manifested their desire to assist and expressed the utmost sympathy at my shrunken appearance.

The feelings which I experienced at the merciful deliverance vouchsafed to me by the Almighty can never be expressed in words. Such feelings are paramount. I was, however, not insensible to the goodwill of my dependants. They made up a bed for me in my *palker gherry*, the first on which I had lain for a length of time, and I lay down to rest amidst their prodigal congratulations.

The ladies were most kindly treated by the 8th or King's Regiment, the mess-room of which was given up for the accommodation of those who would accept of it. Tents were pitched for everybody, and quickly occupied.

The Dilkoosha Palace stands upon an eminence, in the midst of a fine park. Such are its natural advantages, that it presents a most favourable position for an army of occupation of about fifteen thousand men of all arms, which would be no more than an adequate force. Short as our stay was here, it was marked by an event of the most mournful character, which brought sorrow and consternation to every heart, even to the coldest.

Here, on the 24th November, the good, the great Havelock breathed his last. Of him it may in truth be said, that he "fought the good fight." Firm and decided, courteous, urbane, and gentle, he united the fire and spirit of the warrior to the temperance and moderation of the Christian. His every action was ruled by the strictest sense of duty, his valour was only equalled by his prudence, and his goodness was transcendent; but no praise can do justice to virtues such as his. On the succeeding day, his remains were followed to the grave by the commander-in-chief and members of the staff. Sincere was the grief with which I beheld the earth close above him, her most honoured son. The mournful impression cannot be easily effaced; but words are vain.

In addition to the prize property originally under my supervision, on Tuesday, the 24th of November, I was placed in special charge of the Lucknow treasure and crown jewels, but without even being allowed a guard for this arduous and highly responsible duty. Only a sergeant's party of Sikhs was in attendance upon me. I did not, however, miss our soldiers, and found the natives alert and active.

The force marched to the Alum Bagh, in two divisions, and I was attached to the first, under Brigadier-General Grant. The cold weather was favourable to our march, which we pursued briskly, and with the good fortune of not meeting with any impediment in our route.

On Friday, the 27th of November, we pursued our march to Bunnee, at eleven a.m. It was, however, a most tedious and irksome proceeding. The road was thronged with carts, and there was no baggage-staff to move them; there was a total absence of all method or arrangement, and disorder was pre-eminent. By the most intense labour and personal exertion, I succeeded in keeping the tumbrels of treasure and carts together, thirty-six in number being under my charge. Such confusion should not have existed, and might easily have been prevented. One sergeant of cavalry was forwarding the carts, when a corps of sixty at least was indispensable for such a line of baggage. At ten o'clock p.m., we reached Bunnee, and halted two miles in advance.

On Saturday the 28th, at seven a.m., we marched from Bunnee, when the same want of management was conspicuous. The baggage-carts were again allowed to be crowded together, so as effectually to block up the road and obstruct our advance; nor was there a single officer present to put this mass in motion. The order of march was quite unobserved; all regularity was set at defiance. I set to work to correct this mismanagement, cleared the way, got the carts into line, to retain which was a task of much difficulty, permitted the families to precede me, though they had lost their place, and at two o'clock a.m., without a halt, reached the left bank of the Ganges.

We found ourselves just in time to succour Cawnpore, which place, during the absence of the commander-in-chief and his force at Lucknow, had been closely invested by a large force of mutineers from Gwalior. The troops which remained to garrison Cawnpore were engaged with the enemy on the 28th of November, when, it would appear, they met unhappily with a check which obliged them to retire. This check was consequent upon too precipitate an advance. Many were killed and wounded; amongst the former were Brigadier-General Wilson, in command of the valiant 64th, and Major Sterling, of the same corps, both officers of distinguished gallantry. Colonel Woodford, Rifle Brigade, also fell.

On Sunday, November 29th, we re-crossed the bridge of boats, under a heavy fire, having previously crossed it on the advance to relieve Lucknow, the 16th of the foregoing September, without molestation.

All the advantages which we had obtained at Cawnpore, prior to this disastrous affair, have dwindled down to the small space of ground held by our troops. This is entrenched, and serves to cover the bridge, while the picquets of the mutineers face our left flank and are extremely troublesome.

The incessant exertion of the past two days, coupled with my anxiety for the safe arrival of the thirty-six carts of treasure committed to my charge, has completely overcome me. The illness against which I struggled has increased, and the debility and exhaustion consequent on it, demand the repose which it is impossible for me to obtain at present.

In the late affair with the rebels the troops under General Windham, in many instances, have, as might be expected, not proved equal in efficiency to those regiments composed of older men, more inured to the country, and more accustomed to the Asiatic mode of warfare. Their conduct also has not furnished any argument in favour of our present system of camps and depots of instruction—which system, however good it may be in theory, has not been well carried out in practice. That there is a failure in some branch or class is clearly apparent in the want of discipline observable amongst those young soldiers.

From whence has this laxity arisen? And how is it to be extirpated? That it does exist is manifest from the too evident independence of control exhibited by the men, which, it need hardly be remarked, is a most dangerous error. All young officers should bear in mind the importance of their position in relation to their subordinates, and the necessity, for the purpose of inspiring those subordinates with reliance on their judgment and capacity, of studying their profession in all its details, and of presenting in their own persons such an example of steadiness and attention as would leave the soldiers no excuse for want of discipline.

Never can any officer, especially a youth without service, be efficient as a leader, unless he possesses the qualities necessary to beget confidence in the minds of his subordinates.

On the afternoon of the 6th December, a movement was made by the mutineers, whose guns opened in the direction of the camp, and especially on the position held by the commander-in-chief and his staff—but this was soon silenced.

Next morning, after breakfast, our troops attacked the position of the mutineers in force. This they defended by a brisk cannonade, which, however, soon became feeble—while we boldly advanced and drove them out of the bazaar, capturing some guns and holding a more advanced position.

The mutineers were driven to the banks of the river, where they are watched.

Their encampment, containing property plundered from Windham's force, is in our possession. Strange to state, I have recovered one of my trunks, which I left at Cawnpore when advancing to Lucknow. It had, however, been rifled by the enemy, the bottom having been most ingeniously cut out of it to remove its contents; these were chiefly, a stock of linen, a suit of uniform, and some valuables.

December 13th

The communication between this place (Cawnpore) and Allahabad, a distance of a hundred and twenty miles, has not been quite free. A brigade, therefore, is now being sent to occupy posts on the route, and prevent interruption. There has lately been a most delightful change of weather, and it is considerably cooler. Many who have suffered from the pestilential atmosphere and heat of Lucknow, together with its privations, have been greatly benefited by this change. May we all, who have been there, live to bear in mind the merciful deliverance vouchsafed to us by Almighty God, and show forth our gratitude, not only with our lips, but in our lives.

January 10th, 1858

I am labouring under a severe attack of dysentery, caused by past hardships, and further aggravated by present anxiety about the transit of prize property under my charge. This is of great value. It consists of the king's treasure and crown jewels, loosely packed in one hundred and eighteen ammunition boxes, and also of eight barrels of precious stones; all of which were especially entrusted to my care by his excellency the commander-in-chief.

They have been conveyed upon thirty-six carts, sixteen of which are common country *hackeries*, without any proper guard to look after them; but, notwithstanding, by my constant exertion they have all arrived safely. Shaken as it was, my bodily strength was almost unequal to the task, and sank rapidly when there was no longer a demand on my energies.

I was, therefore, obliged to attend to the repeated injunctions and representations of my medical advisers, and prepare for my return to England on sick certificate.

I hoped, ere this, to have joined my regiment; but more rest than was anticipated seems needful after a campaign in India of unexampled severity, and during the unfavourable seasons of the year. I have, however. been rewarded by the thanks of the governor general in council and have been also mentioned in Sir James Outram's despatch as having rendered valuable service.

LEONAUR

ALSO FROM LEONAUR
AVAILABLE IN SOFTCOVER OR HARDCOVER WITH DUST JACKET

A HISTORY OF THE FRENCH & INDIAN WAR *by Arthur G. Bradley*—The Seven Years War as it was fought in the New World has always fascinated students of military history—here is the story of that confrontation.

WASHINGTON'S EARLY CAMPAIGNS *by James Hadden*—The French Post Expedition, Great Meadows and Braddock's Defeat—including Braddock's Orderly Books.

BOUQUET & THE OHIO INDIAN WAR *by Cyrus Cort & William Smith*—Two Accounts of the Campaigns of 1763-1764: Bouquet's Campaigns by Cyrus Cort & The History of Bouquet's Expeditions by William Smith.

NARRATIVES OF THE FRENCH & INDIAN WAR: 2 *by David Holden, Samuel Jenks, Lemuel Lyon, Mary Cochrane Rogers & Henry T. Blake*—Contains The Diary of Sergeant David Holden, Captain Samuel Jenks' Journal, The Journal of Lemuel Lyon, Journal of a French Officer at the Siege of Quebec, A Battle Fought on Snowshoes & The Battle of Lake George.

NARRATIVES OF THE FRENCH & INDIAN WAR *by Brown, Eastburn, Hawks & Putnam*—Ranger Brown's Narrative, The Adventures of Robert Eastburn, The Journal of Rufus Putnam—Provincial Infantry & Orderly Book and Journal of Major John Hawks on the Ticonderoga-Crown Point Campaign.

THE 7TH (QUEEN'S OWN) HUSSARS: Volume 1—1688-1792 *by C. R. B. Barrett*—As Dragoons During the Flanders Campaign, War of the Austrian Succession and the Seven Years War.

INDIA'S FREE LANCES *by H. G. Keene*—European Mercenary Commanders in Hindustan 1770-1820.

THE BENGAL EUROPEAN REGIMENT *by P. R. Innes*—An Elite Regiment of the Honourable East India Company 1756-1858.

MUSKET & TOMAHAWK *by Francis Parkman*—A Military History of the French & Indian War, 1753-1760.

THE BLACK WATCH AT TICONDEROGA *by Frederick B. Richards*—Campaigns in the French & Indian War.

QUEEN'S RANGERS *by Frederick B. Richards*—John Simcoe and his Rangers During the Revolutionary War for America.

ALSO FROM LEONAUR

AFGHANISTAN: THE BELEAGUERED BRIGADE *by G. R. Gleig*—An Account of Sale's Brigade During the First Afghan War.

IN THE RANKS OF THE C. I. V *by Erskine Childers*—With the City Imperial Volunteer Battery (Honourable Artillery Company) in the Second Boer War.

THE BENGAL NATIVE ARMY *by F. G. Cardew*—An Invaluable Reference Resource.

THE 7TH (QUEEN'S OWN) HUSSARS: Volume 4—1688-1914 *by C. R. B. Barrett*—Uniforms, Equipment, Weapons, Traditions, the Services of Notable Officers and Men & the Appendices to All Volumes—Volume 4: 1688-1914.

THE SWORD OF THE CROWN *by Eric W. Sheppard*—A History of the British Army to 1914.

THE 7TH (QUEEN'S OWN) HUSSARS: Volume 3—1818-1914 *by C. R. B. Barrett*—On Campaign During the Canadian Rebellion, the Indian Mutiny, the Sudan, Matabeleland, Mashonaland and the Boer War Volume 3: 1818-1914.

THE KHARTOUM CAMPAIGN *by Bennet Burleigh*—A Special Correspondent's View of the Reconquest of the Sudan by British and Egyptian Forces under Kitchener—1898.

EL PUCHERO *by Richard McSherry*—The Letters of a Surgeon of Volunteers During Scott's Campaign of the American-Mexican War 1847-1848.

RIFLEMAN SAHIB *by E. Maude*—The Recollections of an Officer of the Bombay Rifles During the Southern Mahratta Campaign, Second Sikh War, Persian Campaign and Indian Mutiny.

THE KING'S HUSSAR *by Edwin Mole*—The Recollections of a 14th (King's) Hussar During the Victorian Era.

JOHN COMPANY'S CAVALRYMAN *by William Johnson*—The Experiences of a British Soldier in the Crimea, the Persian Campaign and the Indian Mutiny.

COLENSO & DURNFORD'S ZULU WAR *by Frances E. Colenso & Edward Durnford*—The first and possibly the most important history of the Zulu War.

U. S. DRAGOON *by Samuel E. Chamberlain*—Experiences in the Mexican War 1846-48 and on the South Western Frontier.

LEONAUR

ALSO FROM LEONAUR
AVAILABLE IN SOFTCOVER OR HARDCOVER WITH DUST JACKET

OFFICERS & GENTLEMEN *by Peter Hawker & William Graham*—Two Accounts of British Officers During the Peninsula War: Officer of Light Dragoons by Peter Hawker & Campaign in Portugal and Spain by William Graham .

THE WALCHEREN EXPEDITION *by Anonymous*—The Experiences of a British Officer of the 81st Regt. During the Campaign in the Low Countries of 1809.

LADIES OF WATERLOO *by Charlotte A. Eaton, Magdalene de Lancey & Juana Smith*—The Experiences of Three Women During the Campaign of 1815: Waterloo Days by Charlotte A. Eaton, A Week at Waterloo by Magdalene de Lancey & Juana's Story by Juana Smith.

JOURNAL OF AN OFFICER IN THE KING'S GERMAN LEGION *by John Frederick Hering*—Recollections of Campaigning During the Napoleonic Wars.

JOURNAL OF AN ARMY SURGEON IN THE PENINSULAR WAR *by Charles Boutflower*—The Recollections of a British Army Medical Man on Campaign During the Napoleonic Wars.

ON CAMPAIGN WITH MOORE AND WELLINGTON *by Anthony Hamilton*—The Experiences of a Soldier of the 43rd Regiment During the Peninsular War.

THE ROAD TO AUSTERLITZ *by R. G. Burton*—Napoleon's Campaign of 1805.

SOLDIERS OF NAPOLEON *by A. J. Doisy De Villargennes & Arthur Chuquet*—The Experiences of the Men of the French First Empire: Under the Eagles by A. J. Doisy De Villargennes & Voices of 1812 by Arthur Chuquet .

INVASION OF FRANCE, 1814 *by F. W. O. Maycock*—The Final Battles of the Napoleonic First Empire.

LEIPZIG—A CONFLICT OF TITANS *by Frederic Shoberl*—A Personal Experience of the 'Battle of the Nations' During the Napoleonic Wars, October 14th-19th, 1813.

SLASHERS *by Charles Cadell*—The Campaigns of the 28th Regiment of Foot During the Napoleonic Wars by a Serving Officer.

BATTLE IMPERIAL *by Charles William Vane*—The Campaigns in Germany & France for the Defeat of Napoleon 1813-1814.

SWIFT & BOLD *by Gibbes Rigaud*—The 60th Rifles During the Peninsula War.

LEONAUR

ALSO FROM LEONAUR
AVAILABLE IN SOFTCOVER OR HARDCOVER WITH DUST JACKET

OMPTEDA OF THE KING'S GERMAN LEGION *by Christian von Ompteda*—A Hanoverian Officer on Campaign Against Napoleon.

LIEUTENANT SIMMONS OF THE 95TH (RIFLES) *by George Simmons*—Recollections of the Peninsula, South of France & Waterloo Campaigns of the Napoleonic Wars.

A HORSEMAN FOR THE EMPEROR *by Jean Baptiste Gazzola*—A Cavalryman of Napoleon's Army on Campaign Throughout the Napoleonic Wars.

SERGEANT LAWRENCE *by William Lawrence*—With the 40th Regt. of Foot in South America, the Peninsular War & at Waterloo.

CAMPAIGNS WITH THE FIELD TRAIN *by Richard D. Henegan*—Experiences of a British Officer During the Peninsula and Waterloo Campaigns of the Napoleonic Wars.

CAVALRY SURGEON *by S. D. Broughton*—On Campaign Against Napoleon in the Peninsula & South of France During the Napoleonic Wars 1812-1814.

MEN OF THE RIFLES *by Thomas Knight, Henry Curling & Jonathan Leach*—The Reminiscences of Thomas Knight of the 95th (Rifles) by Thomas Knight, Henry Curling's Anecdotes by Henry Curling & The Field Services of the Rifle Brigade from its Formation to Waterloo by Jonathan Leach.

THE ULM CAMPAIGN 1805 *by F. N. Maude*—Napoleon and the Defeat of the Austrian Army During the 'War of the Third Coalition'.

SOLDIERING WITH THE 'DIVISION' *by Thomas Garrety*—The Military Experiences of an Infantryman of the 43rd Regiment During the Napoleonic Wars.

SERGEANT MORRIS OF THE 73RD FOOT *by Thomas Morris*—The Experiences of a British Infantryman During the Napoleonic Wars-Including Campaigns in Germany and at Waterloo.

A VOICE FROM WATERLOO *by Edward Cotton*—The Personal Experiences of a British Cavalryman Who Became a Battlefield Guide and Authority on the Campaign of 1815.

NAPOLEON AND HIS MARSHALS *by J. T. Headley*—The Men of the First Empire.

LEONAUR

ALSO FROM LEONAUR
AVAILABLE IN SOFTCOVER OR HARDCOVER WITH DUST JACKET

BUGEAUD: A PACK WITH A BATON *by Thomas Robert Bugeaud*—The Early Campaigns of a Soldier of Napoleon's Army Who Would Become a Marshal of France.

WATERLOO RECOLLECTIONS *by Frederick Llewellyn*—Rare First Hand Accounts, Letters, Reports and Retellings from the Campaign of 1815.

SERGEANT NICOL *by Daniel Nicol*—The Experiences of a Gordon Highlander During the Napoleonic Wars in Egypt, the Peninsula and France.

THE JENA CAMPAIGN: 1806 *by F. N. Maude*—The Twin Battles of Jena & Auerstadt Between Napoleon's French and the Prussian Army.

PRIVATE O'NEIL *by Charles O'Neil*—The recollections of an Irish Rogue of H. M. 28th Regt.—The Slashers—during the Peninsula & Waterloo campaigns of the Napoleonic war.

ROYAL HIGHLANDER *by James Anton*—A soldier of H.M 42nd (Royal) Highlanders during the Peninsular, South of France & Waterloo Campaigns of the Napoleonic Wars.

CAPTAIN BLAZE *by Elzéar Blaze*—Life in Napoleons Army.

LEJEUNE VOLUME 1 *by Louis-François Lejeune*—The Napoleonic Wars through the Experiences of an Officer on Berthier's Staff.

LEJEUNE VOLUME 2 *by Louis-François Lejeune*—The Napoleonic Wars through the Experiences of an Officer on Berthier's Staff.

CAPTAIN COIGNET *by Jean-Roch Coignet*—A Soldier of Napoleon's Imperial Guard from the Italian Campaign to Russia and Waterloo.

FUSILIER COOPER *by John S. Cooper*—Experiences in the 7th (Royal) Fusiliers During the Peninsular Campaign of the Napoleonic Wars and the American Campaign to New Orleans.

FIGHTING NAPOLEON'S EMPIRE *by Joseph Anderson*—The Campaigns of a British Infantryman in Italy, Egypt, the Peninsular & the West Indies During the Napoleonic Wars.

CHASSEUR BARRES *by Jean-Baptiste Barres*—The experiences of a French Infantryman of the Imperial Guard at Austerlitz, Jena, Eylau, Friedland, in the Peninsular, Lutzen, Bautzen, Zinnwald and Hanau during the Napoleonic Wars.

LEONAUR

ALSO FROM LEONAUR
AVAILABLE IN SOFTCOVER OR HARDCOVER WITH DUST JACKET

THE RELUCTANT REBEL by William G. Stevenson—A young Kentuckian's experiences in the Confederate Infantry & Cavalry during the American Civil War..

BOOTS AND SADDLES by Elizabeth B. Custer—The experiences of General Custer's Wife on the Western Plains.

FANNIE BEERS' CIVIL WAR by Fannie A. Beers—A Confederate Lady's Experiences of Nursing During the Campaigns & Battles of the American Civil War.

LADY SALE'S AFGHANISTAN by Florentia Sale—An Indomitable Victorian Lady's Account of the Retreat from Kabul During the First Afghan War.

THE TWO WARS OF MRS DUBERLY by Frances Isabella Duberly—An Intrepid Victorian Lady's Experience of the Crimea and Indian Mutiny.

THE REBELLIOUS DUCHESS by Paul F. S. Dermoncourt—The Adventures of the Duchess of Berri and Her Attempt to Overthrow French Monarchy.

LADIES OF WATERLOO by Charlotte A. Eaton, Magdalene de Lancey & Juana Smith—The Experiences of Three Women During the Campaign of 1815: Waterloo Days by Charlotte A. Eaton, A Week at Waterloo by Magdalene de Lancey & Juana's Story by Juana Smith.

TWO YEARS BEFORE THE MAST by Richard Henry Dana. Jr.—The account of one young man's experiences serving on board a sailing brig—the Penelope—bound for California, between the years1834-36.

A SAILOR OF KING GEORGE by Frederick Hoffman—From Midshipman to Captain—Recollections of War at Sea in the Napoleonic Age 1793-1815.

LORDS OF THE SEA by A. T. Mahan—Great Captains of the Royal Navy During the Age of Sail.

COGGESHALL'S VOYAGES: VOLUME 1 by George Coggeshall—The Recollections of an American Schooner Captain.

COGGESHALL'S VOYAGES: VOLUME 2 by George Coggeshall—The Recollections of an American Schooner Captain.

TWILIGHT OF EMPIRE by Sir Thomas Ussher & Sir George Cockburn—Two accounts of Napoleon's Journeys in Exile to Elba and St. Helena: Narrative of Events by Sir Thomas Ussher & Napoleon's Last Voyage: Extract of a diary by Sir George Cockburn.